Hunting
Open-Country
MULE DEER

A Guide for Taking Western Bucks
with Rifle and Bow

By
Dwight Schuh

Published in the United States of America

Hunting
Open-Country
MULE DEER
A Guide for Taking Western Bucks
with Rifle and Bow

by Dwight Schuh

ISBN No. 0-912299-23-1

FOURTH PRINTING, FEBRUARY 2000

— — — —

Third Printing, September 1994
Second Printing, August 1989
First Printing, February 1985

Published by Sage Press in cooperation with Stoneydale Press.

SAGE PRESS   **STONEYDALE PRESS**
P.O. Box 217   523 Main Street
Nampa, Idaho 83653   Stevensville, Montana 59870

TABLE OF CONTENTS

DEDICATION

My dad Joe Schuh, right, and his friend Scott Warren admire a buck my dad killed in Nevada in 1954. Sights like this stirred my heart and imagination as a young boy and planted the seed for mule deer hunting.

FOREWORD

Some outdoor writers write well enough, but tend to rely on hyperbole and embellishment — rather than shooting skill and hard-earned successes — to turn out salable manuscripts for the various hunting magazines. They've learned a long time ago it's much easier to hit a big game animal with a typewriter key than a well-placed bullet or broadhead. Read their articles and you may be convinced they're knowledgeable, efficient hunters. Meet them, talk to them or hunt with them and you may come away disappointed and disillusioned.

Other writers have talents which are not limited to telling tales and attempting to impress their readers with glowing accounts of their accomplishments. These people are good writers **and** good hunters. Their articles entertain and inform. They tell it as it is. Share a hunting camp with them and you'll generally walk away impressed.

Dwight Schuh is one such writer-hunter.

I can clearly remember the first manuscript I received from Dwight over a decade ago. It was a feature article called "Five Steps to Success," a how-to piece on bowhunting open country mule deer. It enumerated the author's personal five-step success formula, stressing the need for developing a sound hunting plan, perfecting camouflage for the terrain, learning to approach game silently, sharpening broadheads to a razor's edge and shooting accurately under pressure.

Sure, it was pretty basic stuff. But its message was delivered in clear, well-written prose that had a ring of authenticity to it thanks to appropriate anecdotes. An ample selection of professional quality photographs completed the manuscript package.

Impressed, I bought the piece and published it in the October/November 1975 issue of *Bowhunter.* Other Dwight Schuh manuscripts followed and were quickly accepted. Not surprisingly, Dwight's by-line began cropping up in the biggest national outdoor magazines. The talented, prolific wordsmith from Oregon was well on his way to establishing himself as one of America's top outdoor writers.

Over the years, I've met Dwight and come to know him better. Today I admire him not only as a gifted writer but as an ethical bowhunter and a modest man. When asked to write the foreword to this book, I was both pleased and proud to oblige.

Dwight Schuh has spent a tremendous amount of time in the field collecting material for his books and articles. This book, for example, is based on countless hours and many seasons of matching wits with one of North America's premier big game animals. Read it, learn from it and you'll be a better hunters. Emulate its author — from attitude to ability — and you'll be a better person.

M. R. James   *Bowhunter Magazine*
Editor-Publisher   August 1985

Hunting
Open-Country
MULE DEER

A Guide for Taking Western Bucks with Rifle and Bow

My introduction to open-country bowhunting came in 1969 when my long-time friend Don Hummel invited me to go along with him to Hart Mountain in the eastern Oregon desert for the opening weekend of bow season. The idea of bowhunting didn't give me any big thrill, but I'd just got out of the Army and was footloose at the moment, and going along on this hunt seemed like a good way to kill some time. Don loaned me an old 56-pound Bear Cub longbow and some crooked cedar arrows, and instantly I was a bowhunter.

My first sight of Hart Mountain did little to raise my hopes. Most people think of Oregon as a wet state where everyone has web feet, but in reality two-thirds of the state is desert, and Hart Mountain lies at the core of that desert. As Don and I topped out on the mountain, I thought this had to be a joke. Sagebrush stretched as endless as waves on the ocean. Except for a few scattered clumps of mahogany on the higher ridges and some aspen groves in the draws, this place virtually had no trees, and the sagebrush wasn't high enough to hide a badger. I doubted in my heart that deer could survive here, and even if they could, a bowhunter obviously couldn't get within range.

Don and I set up camp in an aspen grove that night, and in the dark the next morning we groped blindly up a shallow draw, the fragrance of sage rich in our nostrils. Don whispered, "Sit there," and disappeared into the darkness to take a stand farther uphill.

My first sight of country like this nearly scared me away before I learned the beauties. "Bowhunt for deer out here?" I thought. Now that I've discovered the hidden secrets of open-country, I feel right at home. This camp will never compete with the Hilton, but it's smack in the heart of big-buck country, and that's good enough for me.

Many sounds and smells scratched at my senses, and I tried to fit them together like a jigsaw puzzle to create an image of what might appear with the coming of light. I peered back and forth, trying to see things only an owl could see. In particular I tried to make out the source of a crunch, crunch on gravel across the draw. "Hunters," I thought. But somehow the footfalls seemed too careful, and I could hear no whispering.

Slowly gray light began to pull together pieces of the desert puzzle. To the right a stringer of dark green aspen trees with snow-white trunks snaked up a draw, and on the ridge behind me, as barren and stark as a crater of the moon, two hunters silhouetted against the glowing eastern horizon whispered quietly but distinctly in the still, pure air. The crunching of gravel continued on the far side of my draw, and staring through the binoculars, I began to make out charcoal forms against a dark, rocky hillside. Four deer!

Daylight was coming fast now, and soon I could define antlers, all with four points to the side, all 2 feet wide or wider. I whined and quivered like a retriever watching a flock of ducks, but that was only the start. Before that morning was out I'd counted 17 bucks as big or bigger than those, along with countless smaller bucks and does. With my primitive equipment and even more primitive knowledge of using it, I was no threat to any of those deer, but in my first three hours of bowhunting, I'd seen more big bucks than I'd seen in 15 years of rifle hunting. What an experience! I was hooked.

Since then I've bowhunted in most of the western states, and I'm happy to report that that first day was only a foretaste of finer things to come. Bowhunting for deer in the West promises the finest hunting opportunities available today.

SOME WORDS ABOUT THIS BOOK

Originally I conceived this strictly as a book on mule deer hunting, and that's still the central focus. But over the past few years, as my hunting horizons have continued to expand, I've learned that whitetails in northern Idaho, Coues whitetails in southern Arizona, and blacktails along the Coast Range of California and Oregon, can be hunted in much the same way as the mule deer of Nevada, Utah, Colorado and Montana. As a result this project has evolved into a book about a hunting system more than a book just about mule deer hunting. It applies most widely to mule deer because of their penchant for open country and their wide distribution, but it can be adapted to all deer of the mountainous West. Thus the subtitle, "Open-Country Bucks."

Along these same lines, the title implies that this book applies only to bowhunting, but that's not fully true. Much of the background has come from archery seasons, and bowhunting is the focus, but deer lore is deer lore, and most lessons from bowhunting apply to rifle hunting, too.

Fred Bear, possibly the most famous bowhunter of the 20th Century, once told me he thought one of the great things about bowhunting was that you could learn so much from each experience. For every one opportunity a rifle hunter gets at deer, he pointed out, a bowhunter will get 10 before he actually fills a tag. As a result, bowhunting is ideal for extensive research into the ways of deer, and the knowledge gained applies to all hunting methods, not just archery. That's why this book has some good things to say to all deer hunters, not just hard-core bowhunters.

THE COMPLETE INCOMPLETE BOOK

In the past 10 or 12 years, I've devoured seemingly every book ever written about deer hunting. Like most hunters I was originally attracted to those called "The Complete Book of...." And why not? One complete book should answer all your questions about deer hunting, so you should never have to buy another book on the subject.

After reading a half-dozen "complete" books, however, I realized something — none was complete. Each one tried to cover so much ground in an attempt to be all things to all hunters, it skimmed over each topic lightly and became nothing to nobody.

I don't pretend to know anything about deer drives or tree stands or rifle ballistics or the love life of whitetails in Ohio, so I'll leave those topics for somebody who does know about them. The better part of my deer hunting life has been devoted to bowhunting for western bucks, primarily mule deer, on foot, just me and the deer, one-on-one, in the hinterlands of the West's remote and rugged backcountry. That's the kind of hunting I know, and that's the kind of hunting I've written about here. For the record, then, consider this an incomplete book on deer hunting. It covers only the best of the best.

On the other hand, because the scope is narrow, I've taken liberty to expand each aspect completely. You'll find few other books that treat the subject of optics and game spotting as thoroughly as this one does, and you'll probably never find another with the detail given here on stalking big game.

In addition I've covered important side aspects of hunting the wide-open West — clothing adapted to extremes of hot and cold, camping gear and methods built for the rough terrain and climates inhabited by mule deer, tips for meat care in hot weather and wilderness situations, suggestions on gearing your archery tackle to western hunting conditions, and so forth. In short, this book pretty well covers every detail of bowhunting for open-country bucks.

And despite a seemingly narrow theme, it has remarkably broad application. Bowhunting for open-country deer may offer greater opportunity than any other single type of big game hunting. Well, weighed against the prospects for whitetails in some central and eastern states where seasons range from three to five months long and the bag limit is five deer or more, that may be questionable. But in the context of western hunting, no other hunting endeavor can match open-country bowhunting for sheer opportunity, in terms of both time and range.

As I'll point out in more detail later, western bowhunting seasons offer an unending array of possibilities beginning in mid-July and extending through January. Open-country habitats, from desert to prairie to alpine mountains, are nearly unlimited, and in addition, my approach to hunting, which emphasizes the use of high-power optics, can be applied universally to virtually any situation including the deep woods of brush-loving deer.

So even though *Hunting Open-Country Mule Deer* seems to cover an esoteric subject with limited application, it actually draws on one of the most universal and widely applicable hunting systems available today. Come to think of it, given the detail on each aspect of the subject and wide potential for its use, this may truly be the complete book of deer hunting.

THE PURPOSE

If you've never hunted the West, I honestly think this book will equip you with the knowledge and confidence to plan your own western hunt and to kill deer from the beginning. You won't need to go through a period of grace. If you've bowhunted extensively for deer, you'll still find some useable ideas here.

But expounding on the nuts and bolts of hunting isn't my sole purpose.

Hunting embodies more than technique. A magazine editor once reminded me that hunting is 20 percent doing and 80 percent emotion and that writers should try to match that ratio. Maybe he was right. Sure we read to become better hunters, but in the final analysis, the details that live in the minds and hearts of hunters are the feelings and emotions generated by wild encounters. For that reason, I've tried to capture the emotional essence of deer hunting as well as the technique. If you've hunted bucks of the open-country West, I hope, as you read this book, you'll say, "Ah, yes, I've been there!" Even if you never hunt mule deer or never pick up a bow and arrow, I hope you'll come away saying, "Man, what an experience."

THE DEER AND THE COUNTRY

Mule deer and western hunting in general seem to capture the minds and hearts of most American hunters the way no other endeavor can. That's apparent in the fact that few western hunters head east to hunt whitetails, but many eastern hunters migrate west each fall to hunt mule deer. That's not to put down whitetails or the eastern environment, or even to compare those with the West, only to point out that there is a difference. Apparently the West and the deer that live there offer qualities found nowhere else.

SIZE. In part it could be the sheer size of mule deer. Not that every mule deer grows to awesome proportions, but the occasional buck does, and every hunter dreams of spotting that monster at least once in a lifetime. You don't hear hunters rave on so much when they spot lots of deer, but just wait until one spots Old Mossyhorns, and you'll never hear the end of it. Thirty-inches is the fabled size that every hunter craves to

Even an average buck like this silhouetted against the endless blue western sky can capture your imagination and build dreams that will last forever.

see, and maybe it's dreaming of the 30-inch buck that draws hunters all the way from New York to Wyoming.

But even if a hunter never sees such a buck, his appetites for enormity can be satisfied in mule deer territory. In the clear air and uncluttered horizons that are the West, even the average buck silhouetted in black profile against a blazing red sunrise or an infinite blue sky becomes an impressive creature that cannot be forgotten.

CHALLENGE. Many western hunters who've pursued whitetails, mountain sheep, elk, and all the other grand and celebrated species, still revere mule deer above them all. You hear all these stories about how mule deer run out there and stop and wait for you to shoot, and that may even be true with young bucks, and it may do you some good if you're packing a rifle.

But you won't see many really big bucks doing it, and even if you did, it wouldn't help you much as a bowhunter. Mule deer, like antelope and other open-country game, are vulnerable to high-power rifles, but the qualities that make them easy pickings for rifle hunters magnify the challenge for bowhunters. Most hunters, including rifle hunters, who've really dedicated themselves to mule deer maintain that a big old mule deer buck may be the toughest trophy of all, the supreme challenge. I have to agree. In good country, just killing A deer may not be all that tough, but killing THE deer takes some doing.

And even if killing him isn't the toughest challenge, getting to him might be. Most anybody can hunt places where the biggest whitetails come from. It might take some hunting savvy to kill an Iowa cornfield buck, and it certainly takes patience, but it doesn't demand much physical endurance. You don't even have to be in shape.

But if you plan to take big mule deer year after year, you'd better be in shape or you might die. Sure the odd trophy buck is shot in an alfalfa field or next to a farmer's barn, but don't stake your hopes to find one in such places. Few other animals, including elk or sheep, can lead you to more rugged, frightening, lonely, isolated, beautiful, awesome reaches of North American landscape than can mule deer. Find a terrible-looking piece of real estate, and 10 to 1 a big buck lives there, if for no other reason than no hunter has been tough enough to get to him. There's your challenge.

THE PIONEER SPIRIT. Maybe that aspect — the country — is the thing that really draws hunters from across the U.S. to mule deer land. Hunting these animals ranks as an experience unto itself. Even if you go all day without spotting one buck, you've still experienced something that stirs your soul.

One writer said bowhunting for whitetails is the best there is. Indeed, whitetails do have a universal appeal that qualifies them as great game animals. They live within reach of most hunters and can be hunted on a shoestring, and no animal is more beautiful than a sleek whitetail.

Still, the whitetail world lacks qualities that distinguish good hunting from great. Maybe it's isolation or wildness, loneliness, freedom, grandeur. Oh, you'll find whitetails in wild, inspiring country, say in New England, or Canada, or untapped Montana, but for the most part whitetails are deer of the bottomlands, farms and woodlots, deer that have adapted to man and his environment. They're civilized deer.

Not so mule deer. They inhabit lonely places, the last bastions of wilderness, the few places where you can actually get lost or stranded, where you can wander for a week or more without seeing another soul, where you can experience some of the sights and feelings the early mountain men and pioneers must have experienced. Mule deer live where you don't have to ask permission to hunt.

A few years after my introduction to bowhunting, I shot a small buck at Hart Mountain. This forked horn was hardly the buck I'd dreamed of killing, which could have detracted from the hunt, but as I sat on a cliff, skinning that buck, the enormity of the experience dispelled any disappointment. Wind hissing up through the cliffs buffeted my hair, and my camouflage shirt flapped like sheets on a clothes line. The smell of sage and juniper was as aromatic and alluring as a woman's perfume.

From mysterious depths of the shadowed cliffs 2,000 feet below, a pair of golden eagles soared into view, at first only brown specks floating in the sunlight. I put aside the skinning knife to stare. The eagles held their broad wings rigid, yet magically they rose higher and higher until they were at eye level with me, tilting their curious heads to inspect this strange predator kneeling beside his prey. They continued to rise until they'd become mere specks against the glaring sun. Then drawing in their wings, they swooped past my cliff like lightning bolts to vanish thousands of feet below into the black shadows of the cliffs.

I returned to my work. Tallow and flecks of red meat coated my hands. The deer was fat. I'd shot this buck the afternoon before, at 40 yards, as he lay bedded under a cliff. Night had fallen by the time I'd gutted the deer, so I'd hiked the 3 miles back to camp, stumbling across the black sage flats and scab rock, and had returned in the dark this morning with my packframe. Long hours and long miles had drained my mind and body, but the satisfaction of accomplishment overshadowed fatigue or second thoughts. I felt a pioneer pride, something any self-sufficient person who provides for himself and his family must feel.

This setting exemplified mule deer hunting for me, a pursuit that takes a hunter to high, wild and lonely places; worlds where eagles, wind, sun and cliffs reign; worlds that strain a man to his limits yet promise him freedom and solitude, accomplishment, pride and satisfaction. The essence of hunting deer of the wide-open West doesn't lie necessarily in the taking of an animal but in the experience of hunting. Whenever and wherever you hunt bucks of the West, savor it; it's too good to take lightly. Remember, this is the best.

DWIGHT SCHUH
May 1985

CHAPTER 1

PLANNING A HUNT

In the past I've written a lot about planning a hunt and possibly have overworked the subject, but it's just too important to ignore. Hunting technique and knowledge are important but they aren't the basis for good hunting. Even a bungler can shoot the heck out of deer in a good spot, but a great bowhunter will be hard pressed to get much but exercise in poor country. In recent years I've killed some game, and I attribute my success not so much to any particular hunting skill as to the places I've hunted. In some of those areas, it would be amazing if a person DIDN'T kill a deer.

Now, I'm not about to tell you right where my best spots are because then we'd all end up there and none of us would have a good hunt. But I will tell you how I've found these places, and then you can go out and find your own.

SELF-GUIDED

Hire an outfitter. That seems to be the standard advice of some writers, but I think just making a blanket statement like that is baloney. For some persons and some kinds of hunting that might be valid advice. Elk, for example, are relatively difficult to hunt so a beginner would do well to seek guidance the first time around. And besides, it's awful nice to have a packer and his horses handy once you get an elk on the ground.

But deer aren't elk. Using the methods described in this book, you can find deer with no problem on your own, and anyone with a little grit can pack a deer. If you just like the idea of going along on a horseback hunt and don't care a great deal about how you hunt or what you kill, then by all means go on a guided hunt. And certainly if you're a beginner and need someone to show you the basics of bowhunting and finding animals, then an experienced guide who has worked with bowhunters can start you on the right foot.

But if you know bowhunting fundamentals and have some initiative to do things for yourself, you can do just as well or better on your own. I've taken guided hunts for bear and elk but never for deer, and I don't feel deprived. Doing it on your own allows a lot more flexibility in time, place and method, which can be the essence of good hunting. Besides, doing it on you own will save you some money, and it breeds real satisfaction.

CHOOSING THE COUNTRY

You can pick hunting country two ways — either find one good spot and return there year after year, or look for new places each year. Each has its strong points. If you've found a good place to hunt and are happy with it, then your chances for killing a really good buck are probably best right there. You don't have to continually re-invent the wheel every time you go hunting. And besides, there's something comforting and friendly about returning to spots filled with memories of past hunts.

But maybe you've never hunted open-country bucks before and are just now setting out to find your hunting paradise. Or maybe you're like me and just like to try on new country for size. I'm a little like the bear who goes over the mountain just to see what he can see, so I'm continually looking for new spots, hoping to find the most fabulous deer hunting on earth. Sometimes this philosophy pays off and I strike it rich, and sometimes I strike out and kick myself for not just hunting one of my old reliables.

At any rate, if you're looking to new country, and don't have time or money actually to look over a number of places personally, your only hope for a good hunt is research. Over the past 10 years I've planned a couple-dozen out-of-state hunts, and most of them have surpassed my fondest expectations. My friend Mike Cupell and I backpacked into a desert range one August, and the first night from camp, before we'd even got our tents set up, we'd glassed 25 bucks. That has been typical. An occasional hunt has bombed on me, but rarely, and in virtually all cases, I can correlate the quality of the hunt with the extent of my research. A lot of research, good hunt; little research, bad hunt.

RESEARCH

Finding good spots begins with curiosity. That means you read books and magazines to pick up ideas. Archery magazines have all kinds of stories about bowhunting in western states, and reading these will plant some seeds, but don't make the mistake of reading just bowhunting articles. General outdoors magazines carry all kinds of rifle articles, as well as where-to guides in their regional pages. Don't ignore these. Maybe you're not a rifle hunter, but that doesn't matter. The country doesn't change from rifle to bow season, and the same deer that existed there during rifle season live there during bow season. Any book or article that describes a piece of country can give you some ideas about the terrain, vegetation and quality of deer.

One of the biggest problems with magazine articles, especially about deer hunting, is that they're heavily weighted toward only a few states, especially Colorado and Utah. Those are good states, but don't think for a minute they're the only ones. Actually, bowhunting opportunities are meager in these states compared to some others. I don't recall ever reading about an eastern bowhunter traveling to my home state of Oregon to hunt, but you wouldn't believe.... Well, never mind about that. You can research that for yourself.

READING THE REGS

To get the full picture, order regulations from every western state. (In Appendix One you'll find a complete list of western game departments along with addresses of public land agencies, a bibliography of useful books, and a list of sample questions that will help you plan a research strategy.)

As you'll discover from the regulations, western bow seasons begin in mid-July with California's coastal blacktail season. The majority of general bow seasons, particularly for mule deer, then open in late August or early September. Seasons are as short as two weeks in some states and up to six weeks in others, and the average is a month. Special late seasons open in October and November, and you'll find some form of bowhunting clear till the end of January with Arizona's late mule deer and Coues whitetail seasons. With that kind of range, you can just about pick your time, place and conditions.

EARLY SEASONS. As a rule of thumb, the earlier in the year you hunt, the more deer you'll see, which is true for a couple of reasons. First, bucks still have velvet on their antlers in August. Velvet antlers are tender, so bucks avoid brush and timber that will bang up their antlers and hang out in relatively open terrain where they're easy to see.

In most cases, a buck's antlers begin to harden in late August, and they start shedding velvet about September 1. Some years it seems every buck I've seen on August 30 still had velvet, and two days later they've all been rubbed. Consistently, by the first week in September virtually all bucks have polished their antlers. You can still spot plenty of deer at this time, particularly in lightly hunted areas, but with any hunting pressure bucks are likely to dive into brush cover, and then they'll be harder to spot.

One other thing to consider is whether you want to shoot a buck in

Western bow seasons kick off with California's early blacktail season, which opens in mid-July. Arizona hunter Mike Cupell traveled to California to kill this forked horn. This buck is in velvet, as most bucks will be at this time of year.

velvet. Most western bowhunters take bucks in velvet for granted, but easterners might not. A friend from Pennsylvania came out to hunt with me one year, and he almost considered it a sacrilege to shoot a buck in velvet. If you feel that way, plan your hunt after September 1 and you'll be okay.

You'll also see the most deer early because deer are most active in summer, which contradicts popular opinion. Many hunters reason that in winter deer need lots of energy to stay warm so they'll eat more then and will feed for longer periods than they do in warm weather. Actually, just the opposite is true. In winter, the metabolic rate of deer slows down. In essence, the animals go into "semi-hibernation." Their bodily processes slow down, so they need less food, and they remain motionless for long periods to conserve energy.

In contrast, during summer they're putting on fat for the coming fall and winter, and bucks are growing antlers and does are nursing fawns. That's when energy demands are highest, and as a result that's when deer feed for the longest periods of time. It's common in August to see animals feeding as late as 10 a.m. and then again from early afternoon until dark. By mid-September, when their antlers are hard, metabolism slows down, and they become less active and visible. That doesn't mean you can't spot enough bucks in September and October for a good hunt because you can, but if you want to see LOTS of deer, hunt as early as possible, in August and early September, when the bucks are in velvet and are feeding continually.

LATE SEASONS. Of course, early general seasons don't offer the only good hunting, and you can find plenty of great opportunities by studying regulations. Idaho, Washington and other states hold November and December hunts for both whitetails and mule deer. During normal years, heavy snow forces deer onto restricted winter ranges where they become extremely concentrated and visible and a bowhunter can have exceptional hunting, especially for big, timber bucks you might never see earlier.

RUT HUNTING. Some of these later seasons also take place during the rut. In most states the rut falls in November and you can see some fabulous deer at this time. A number of western Oregon blacktail units, for example, are open to bowhunting in November, and the chance for taking a record book animal during this time is excellent. In the Southwest, desert mule deer and Coues whitetails rut from late December through January, and both Arizona and New Mexico traditionally hold bow seasons during this time for these species.

SPECIAL SEASONS. In some areas, because of nearby urban development, or perhaps just because of tradition, special units have been set aside for bowhunting only. Oregon, Montana and other states have such archery-only areas. In some of these, the seasons extend well beyond general statewide archery seasons, and some special archery units produce huge bucks because rifle hunters never have a chance to crop them off.

Also keep your eye open for limited-tag units. In all reality, rifle hunting pressure, not bow, dictates the quality of a deer herd, so in particular look for units where rifle tags are limited but bow tags aren't. Don't mistakenly assume tags are limited because there aren't any deer. In wide-open regions where deer are especially vulnerable to high-power rifles, tags have been cut back to improve deer numbers and quality. That's the case statewide in Nevada and Arizona and in some desert units in Oregon. In some localities, tags are limited partly to minimize conflicts between hunters and landowners. Colorado has gained its reputation primarily on the basis of its West Slope deer herds, but the prairie counties east of Denver, where tags are limited, have the highest percentage of mature bucks and offer excellent hunting for both mule deer and whitetails.

I can't prescribe any exact formula for choosing a hunt period and location. It depends on when you can hunt, how much time and money you've got, and what you're looking for in the way of a buck. But a close look at regulations will give you some ideas to build on.

Some states hold late seasons when deer have been forced onto winter ranges, and some of these seasons fall during the rut. When bucks are chasing does, as this one is doing, you have a good chance of taking an extra big buck. (Photo by Pat Miller.)

THE MOON. Hunting regulations and the moon don't have much to do with each other, but the moon has something to do with timing of your hunt, so I'll mention it briefly here. One of the questions hunters most often ask me is: "Should I plan my hunt during the dark phase of the moon?"

Some hunters reason that deer can see better at night when the moon is bright, so the animals will bed earlier during the day and be less visible. That reasoning first assumes that a deer needs moonlight to see at night. Biologists who've studied movement patterns of deer tell me these animals have excellent night vision and can move and feed just as well on dark nights as on bright nights. So a dark moon phase isn't a hindrance, and a bright moon isn't a help.

Also, there may be reason for deer NOT to feed during bright nights. Researcher Lee Gladfelter, in extensive studies on the nighttime movements of whitetails, found deer actually were more active on cloudy and moonless nights. He thought it might be because deer feel more secure in the open during dark nights because they're less visible to predators. If anything, then, this suggests you're better off to hunt during a dark moon. I can't document the effects one way or the other. I've had fantastic deer spotting during full moon periods and equally good following dark nights. My advice is, don't worry about it.

MAPS

Curiosity may be the very foundation of planning a good hunt. It starts with reading, but it extends to maps. One of my favorite pastimes is sitting around perusing maps, looking for mountain ranges or wilderness areas where possibly no one else has ever hunted. Some of my best hunts have resulted from vicarious hunting trips taken on maps. When a particular mountain or ridge catches my eye, I'll follow up and ask a few locals what they know about it. Sometimes these ideas flop, but often they pan out big.

To start with, large scale maps like U.S. Geological Survey quadrangle maps won't do you much good because they don't cover enough area. You need those once you've chosen a specific place to hunt, but for general looking, smaller scale maps that cover more territory are better. The U.S.G.S. publishes state and regional topographic maps, which cover lots of country and give you a good idea of elevations and general terrain. These, along with U.S. Forest Service maps of national forests, serve as good starting points.

Most of the west's best deer hunting takes place on National Forest land, although Bureau of Land Management (BLM) lands also offer plenty of good hunting in some states. Private land holds potential, too, and if you have a contact who can get you onto a good ranch, or you want to pay a trespass fee to hunt private land, fair enough. But don't feel left out if you can't hunt private land. Public domain holds 90 percent of the best deer hunting in the West.

LOOK HIGH. To get anything out of maps, you have to know what to look for. Speaking very generally, you'll find the most bucks during early general seasons at high elevations. Mind you, there are many exceptions, but that's a good starting point, and it applies to most major mountain ranges and Great Basin desert country.

TIMBERED MOUNTAINS. The two major mountain chains are the Rockies and the Cascades and Sierra Nevada. Actually the Cascade Range, which runs from northern Washington south through Oregon and into northern California, and the Sierra Nevada, form one major range, but it changes names near Mt. Lassen south of Susanville, California. The way I understand it, the Cascades are volcanic and the Sierras are granite. Whatever the geology, the deer act about the same. They live high in summer.

The Rocky Mountains are complex and spread many fingers and tributary ranges into Idaho, Montana, Wyoming, Utah, Colorado and New Mexico. It would take an entire book to describe every aspect so I can only speak in general terms here. In addition to these major ranges there are other smaller independent mountain chains such as the Blue Mountains in Washington and Oregon, and Wasatch in Utah.

In general these are all forested mountain ranges where timber harvest plays an important part of local economies. Most have designated wilderness areas of one size or another, most of them reach above timberline, and in most, deer migrate seasonally from high-elevation summer ranges to low-elevation winter ranges.

In August and September, during general bow seasons, you'll find most deer at or above timberline. You can't judge by elevation alone because timberline at northern latitudes, in Oregon and Washington, northern Idaho and western Montana is only 6,000 to 8,000 feet elevation. The farther south you go the higher timberline gets until it's nearly 12,000 feet in Colorado. Regardless of elevation, wherever you hunt in major forested mountain ranges you'll find bucks in alpine country near timberline during early bow seasons.

DESERT COUNTRY. The Great Basin is a vast expanse of land that takes in most of eastern Oregon and southern Idaho, all of Nevada and part of northern Arizona, and it extends east and west from California into Utah. The predominant plant in Great Basin desert is sagebrush, and the terrain typically consists of sweeping, low elevation basins divided by high, isolated mountain ranges. Again, generally speaking, elevation dictates deer distribution, because, as Utah biologist Grant Jense pointed out, elevation essentially means water — low country is dry, high country has ample water. That's why in most desert mountain ranges, you'll find the highest concentrations of deer at the highest elevations. Many desert ranges are higher than 10,000 feet, and most of the deer live in a band between 8,000 and 10,000 feet.

However, that's not universally true. Mule deer live throughout the

Most western states hold general bow seasons in August and September, and in the high mountains at that time you'll find most bucks at or above timberline. Here Ken Barr marvels at the number of deer tracks in this seemingly barren alpine terrain.

Great Basin deserts wherever there's adequate water, and primarily that means above 6,000 feet. In some places rugged, prominent mountain ranges are replaced by sloping sage plateaus and flats, and anywhere you find elevations above 6,000 feet, you'll most likely find at least a few mule deer. Some of the biggest bucks are taken from little isolated ridges or pockets overlooked by most hunters. Deer aren't numerous in these places, but because most people ignore them in favor of high-density deer areas, some old desert bucks get big.

THE SOUTHWEST. The Sonoran desert of southern New Mexico, Arizona and California, presents exactly the opposite situation. Here

Rocky Mountain mule deer give way to desert mule deer, and these deer inhabit low-elevation desert floors. Even though many of the mountains in southern Arizona rise to elevations higher than 9,000 feet, most desert mule deer live at elevations of 2,500 to 5,000 feet out on the desert flats and foothills. Coues whitetails share the same region, and they occupy the higher elevations. Their range starts at about 5,000 feet and extends to the tops of the mountain ranges.

That's just opposite of the situation in the northern Rockies, where mule deer live in the highest peaks along with bighorn sheep and mountain goats, and northern whitetails, which share the same region, stick to the bottomlands.

PRAIRIE. Another kind of country ideal for open-country tactics is what I generally lump together as prairie and badlands. The western edge of several Great Plains states — the Dakotas, Nebraska, Kansas, Oklahoma — along with the eastern halves of Montana, Wyoming and Colorado, consist of prairie country, interspersed with badlands and breaks. Mostly this is flat or rolling country with elevations ranging from 3,000 to 6,000 feet. Mule deer live throughout the entire region in uplands wherever vegetation, in the form of sparse forests or brushlands; or terrain, in the form of breaks or badlands, offer escape cover. Whitetails also are abundant in this region, primarily in creek bottoms and around farmlands in the concealment of willows, cottonwoods and other vegetation.

To plan well, you have to understand the nature of the deer you want to hunt. In most regions, mule deer live high and whitetails live low, but in the Southwest the opposite is true. Here mule deer live in the desert lowlands, where Duwane Adams is glassing, and Coues whitetails live high in the distant mountains.

That's a very brief thumbnail sketch of western deer distribution. Don't take it as law because for everything I've said here you can find an exception. Some of the best mule deer are killed in the middle of the summer in low country where mule deer have no right to live. And on and on. Nevertheless, this gives you a broad picture, and it makes one point: In order to plan a hunt, you have to understand the nature of deer in a general region. You can't just say they live high or low. It depends on the region. With that understanding you can study maps intelligently.

OTHER PEOPLE

By now, you probably have some idea of WHEN you want to hunt and in WHICH STATE, and you're starting to narrow it down to a few general mountain ranges or drainages. Now you can start investigating the quality of deer you'll find in each. In some cases, you can get statistics from game departments that show where the most deer are killed, hunting success rates and so forth. Every state publishes a book full of such statistics, and from some states you can get these easily. Colorado goes out of its way to help hunters by selling a book called *COLORADO BIG GAME HARVEST* (see address in Appendix 3). California has regularly published findings from latest big game surveys to show hunters current herd conditions. Other states compile data in books but don't make these generally available to the public, but if you talk to the right person you might borrow or beg such a volume. Some states don't seem to care whether they help hunters at all.

If you can come up with harvest statistics and survey data, study them to get some general ideas. They'll show you which units have the highest harvest, the level of hunter success, average size of bucks and so forth, but don't take all this as law. Statistics might not lie, but they sure can mislead you, and you have to interpret them to draw any valid conclusions. After I'd written an article on planning a hunt, a biologist in Colorado told me he didn't think it would do the average hunter much good because harvest statistics and buck-doe ratios and all that are just too hard to interpret. His point is well taken and I agree, but I look at all this like the pieces of a puzzle. No one part of the planning process can stand by itself, but if you keep juggling the pieces around, you'll pretty soon see a picture developing.

Personal contacts provide the most reliable pieces of the hunting puzzle. Locals who've observed and hunted a piece of country for years know the deer herds, the weather, the kind of country, and so forth. They can turn the hodge-podge of ideas and facts you've collected into a living, growing picture.

If you want to learn in a hurry, call people personally. I've quit wasting my time writing for information (except for general stuff like regulations). A person who won't take 5 minutes to write a letter will talk for an hour on the phone, and you can pursue a lot more incisive line of questioning during a conversation than you can in a letter. I normally start by talking to local big game biologists, and then I branch out to hunters, foresters and other land managers.

PREPARE YOURSELF. Do some research with maps, regulations and hunting statistics before you start calling locals to ask questions. First, you can't ask intelligent questions if you don't have any knowledge. Second, few people will help somebody just looking for a free lunch. It galls me to have someone call up and ask me to tell them a good hunting spot. Cold turkey. They've done nothing to pay their dues; they want something for nothing. I find myself suddenly ignorant when someone like that calls.

On the other hand, if someone asks specific questions that show he's already done some of his own legwork, I'm willing to contribute some useful information. Sometimes I find myself saying too darned much and wish I'd keep my mouth shut. It all depends on how well prepared the inquirer is. My attitude about this is fairly typical. Most people will help someone who's willing to help himself, but they'll clam up if they think you're trying to take advantage of them.

BIOLOGY. First an area has to have pretty fair numbers of deer for good bowhunting. Sure, you might kill the buck of a lifetime on a small mountain range that supports only 100 deer total, but that's the kind of place for a local who can scout to find those deer.

If you're traveling from a long way you need good numbers of animals to work with, so the first thing to ask about is densities. How many deer live in a particular region? Actually, few people could give you any absolute numbers. A regional biologist who works there might offer an estimate, but that's not all that important. You want to know how many you'll see. If you put in a hard day's hunting, would you see a half-dozen deer? Or 20? Or could you expect to spot at least 50 bucks in a day? Somebody can give you a subjective judgment along those lines.

It's important to ask about deer numbers from year to year. Unlike elk, which maintain relatively stable populations, deer fluctuate. Weather can virtually wipe them out, and where you saw dozens of bucks one year, you might be hard pressed to find a half-dozen the next. That's particularly true in the high-elevation country of the Rocky Mountains where deer are at the mercy of winter weather. Just like quail, their numbers go up and down like a roller coaster. Always ask about the present status of deer herds.

Remember also that deer live in pockets, and that just because a mountain range has lots of deer doesn't mean you'll find them everywhere. Find out what kinds of plants and cover the deer seek during the particular seasons you'll be hunting. Every mountain range has "buck pastures." Looking around in general you might only see a couple of bucks a day, but if you find the right basin or ridge at a given time, you might see a couple of dozen. A biologist gave me a tip about a supposed buck pasture that sounded too good to pass up, so a friend and I planned a hunt there, and the tip turned out to be hot. The first morning we found 80 bucks IN

ONE HERD. We'd never seen so many antlers in one place. That's the kind of sight a little judicious question-asking will produce.

If you're looking for better-than-average bucks, you'll want to ask about the buck-doe ratio. Biologists express the relative number of bucks in a herd as a ratio—the number of bucks per every 100 does—and generally the higher the ratio, the more mature bucks. For example, a deer herd with a ratio of 10 bucks per 100 does will not contain many old bucks; chances are that 80 percent of the bucks killed in such a unit are yearlings. In comparison, if the buck-doe ratio is 40 bucks per 100 does, a high percentage of the bucks killed are mature bucks.

You can find a whopping trophy virtually anywhere, even if the buck-doe ratio is 5 bucks per 100 does. But if you're really serious about killing a trophy, look for high-ratio areas. Any unit with a buck-doe ratio higher than 20 per 100 probably contains enough good bucks to make things interesting, but a ratio higher than 30 bucks per 100 does is even better. You can rest assured you'll see plenty of mature bucks there.

Wherever you hunt in the West, you'll find that deer concentrate in pockets, and some pockets must be considered buck pastures. In the places you might find anywhere from a half-dozen to 100 or bucks hanging out together. This group of seven bucks presents an average scene during late-summer bow seasons.

ISOLATED POCKETS. Even if the overall buck-doe ratio in a unit isn't particularly high, it may be very high in some parts of the range. In one mountain range I've hunted, the overall buck-doe ratio, taken as an average on all winter ranges, is only about 20 per 100, but biologists tell me it's 40 to 50 bucks per 100 does in some wilderness pockets there. In fact, we found the 80-buck herd in that mountain range. Ask specifically about hard-to-reach places where a disproportionate number of bucks might live to old age.

Isolated pockets not only hold more bucks in some cases, but they hold few hunters, and I think competition may have as much to do with good hunting as the number of deer. As you study maps look for roadless drainages or places isolated by cliffs, rivers or other obstacles that might limit the number of hunters. Then investigate these further as you talk to locals. Find out if you could really get away from people there. Over the years I've enjoyed fantastic hunting, and location has been the whole secret. I've sought out places where nobody else would hunt. Even when deer numbers haven't been great, the hunting has been great because I've had the deer there all to myself.

OPEN COUNTRY. Finally, find out what the country looks like. In a nutshell, the more open the better. A couple of years ago while planning a desert hunt, I called a number of biologists and hunters to discuss potentially good areas. Without exception, they suggested areas with dense cover — mountain mahogany, aspens, junipers. Their reasoning was, I suppose, that a bowhunter must get close to deer for good shots, and the denser the timber and brush cover, the better the chances for getting close.

In my mind that's dead wrong. As I'll discuss at length in following chapters, your biggest advantage is to spot deer before they see you. That's so important, it has become the very basis for my bowhunting system. Heavy timber and cover only hamper your efforts. Dense foliage gives deer a much greater advantage over you than it gives you over them. To see deer first, you must get out in the high, wide and open. In planning any hunt, I ask people, "Is this country the kind of place where you can sit on one side of a canyon and spot deer on the other?" If the answer is no, I scratch it right there. But if the answer is yes, and all other aspects sound acceptable, I know I'm on a hot track.

CHAPTER 2

SPOTTING AND STALKING

Our first few years of desert hunting, my friends and I mostly hiked long and hard, trying to see as many deer as possible, hoping to fling a few arrows. We had a lot of hope, energy and enthusiasm, but little direction and a miserable chance for success. We seemed to work on the philosophy — and we weren't the only ones working on this premise — that the more ground we covered the more deer we'd see, and the more deer we saw the better the hunting. We did see deer, all right, although not many for the amount of time and energy we expended, but generally they were bounding through the sage in high gear. Whatever shots we did take were long ones at running deer. We never killed anything.

Well, I may be dumb, but I'm not stupid, and after a couple of seasons like that it struck me that something was wrong. The biggest problem, it seemed, was our lack of a plan. We hunted erratically like dust blown by the wind. We rarely knew where we were going or why we were going there. We just went. Long, hard and hungry. We needed direction.

THE PLAN

With that realization, I first analyzed the records at Hart Mountain and found that overall hunting success, for bucks, does and fawns, was less than 5 percent, which meant my misery had plenty of company. That might have made me feel a little better, but it didn't do much to encourage me. If nobody else could kill these deer, what hope had I?

I asked the refuge manager why success at Hart Mountain was so low.

"Success is always low in the desert because it's hard to get close to deer in this open country," he said.

At face value that seemed logical, but again, it didn't give me much encouragement. Did that mean we were all resigned to a 5 percent level of success? That thought was enough to discourage anybody, and it might have deterred my investigations, too, if it hadn't been for one hopeful discovery. Even though the AVERAGE success was less that 5 percent, a few guys I met had killed good bucks at Hart Mountain nearly every year for 10 years running. Either they'd taken those bucks despite the open country, or they'd taken them BECAUSE of it. I had to found out which it was.

So I interviewed the successful hunters, and to the man they had one thing in common. Method. They'd learned how to make open country work for them. They hunted with binoculars and scopes to spot deer at long range, and when they'd found the buck they wanted, they stalked it. Most wouldn't even leave their cars until they'd located a buck in a stalkable position.

PRACTICING WHAT THEY PREACHED

Armed with this revelation, and after some coaching on how to spot deer, I set out my third year of bowhunting with renewed enthusiasm. It was 1 p.m. the second day of the season when my wife Laura and I sat on a canyon rim to eat lunch. We'd spotted some deer the previous day, as well as that morning, and I'd tried a couple of stalks, but without success. The system hadn't yet proved itself, but it showed promise.

"That looks like a deer lying under a tree down there," Laura said, pointing to a clump of junipers in the bottom of the canyon.

Looking through binoculars I made out a spike buck lying in the shade on the downhill side of a tree, chewing his cud, as calm as a dog by the fireplace. He was no monster, but given my bowhunting record up to that point, and my desperate need for experience, this spike might just be what the doctor ordered.

As Laura sat right there to guide me, I walked around the head of the canyon and came out about 200 yards above the buck. For several minutes I waited there, regaining my breath, watching for a signal from Laura. She didn't move. All systems go.

Slowly I walked down the hillside, glassing ahead for the deer, watching for Laura's signals. The hillside was barren, covered only with gravel and scattered sage. My boots grated loudly, so 100 yards above the buck I slipped them off and went ahead in sock feet, as quiet as a slug on a wet log.

At 40 yards I saw the buck's antlers just beyond his bedding tree. He'd got up to feed. I froze in the open as he walked uphill, feeding toward me. As he came into view, I slowly drew my old 48-pound Wing Thunderbird recurve and released a 2018 shaft. It looked like a good shot but the buck sprinted uphill, seemingly unhurt. Then he turned downhill and I saw a blotch of red on the far side of his chest. On the money. It had gone clear through. The buck churned 75 yards downhill and piled up. My first deer with a bow. I'd found a plan.

CHOOSING THE METHOD

It seems to me you can choose a hunting method one of two ways. Either you can hunt under varied circumstances and choose a hunting method — stand, drive, still-hunt, whatever — that will work there; or you can choose one hunting method and find conditions where that method will work. I've chosen the second.

That might seem rather narrow minded, but a conversation with Duwane Adams, an outfitter and successful hunter in Arizona who specializes in trophy mule deer and Coues whitetails, only strengthened my convictions. Duwane hunts by one method — he sets up a big pair of binoculars on a tripod and sits and looks through the binoculars until he spots the deer he wants. Then he stalks it.

As we sat on a rolling desert hillside late one afternoon, I watched Duwane spot deer after deer. His ability seemed uncanny, and it was exciting to see so much game in country most hunters would consider barren. Because of his success as a hunter, and as an outfitter with a reputation for helping his clients kill outstanding bucks, I figured Duwane had a bag of tricks to cover every situation.

Not far above us, the rolling desert gave way to jagged foothills, and above that the timbered mountains took over. That high country intrigued me. With all the cover up there, it seemed that's where the big bucks would be, so I assumed Duwane hit those mountains hard.

"Duwane, how would you hunt up there in those thick oak trees?" I said.

He glanced away from his binoculars only for an instant. "I don't," he said. "I have to hunt where I can see. Spotting is the way to kill big bucks."

SPOT-AND-STALK

Adopting one method to the exclusion of others might seem to greatly limit the breadth of your hunting, but it doesn't really. The application in prairie, desert and alpine country should be obvious, but even in heavily forested country, and for species other than mule deer, spot-and-stalk hunting works quite well, thank you. I've hunted whitetails during late bow seasons in northern Idaho and made it work there, and I've applied it successfully many times in the brushy blacktail environs along the Pacific Coast. It's just a matter of locating clearcuts, natural meadows and brush patches, open bowls and other conditions that allow you to see from one side of a draw or canyon to the other.

Even a lot of mule deer country is anything but spacious, yet the deer here can be spotted and stalked. An experience in Oregon's Wallowa

Duwane Adams, a skilled trophy deer hunter from Arizona, thinks spotting is the only way to hunt big bucks. He simply won't hunt in country where he can't spot deer from long range with his 15X60 Zeiss binoculars.

Mountains illustrates my point. In a heavily timbered basin I found some great deer sign, but I couldn't find the bucks. The place was a jungle and without question the deer were seeing or hearing me before I could see them. It seemed futile.

But I felt sure a good buck lived there, so I figured it was time to try the spot-and-stalk method in country that could hardly be called "open." I climbed a high cliff and sat on a bare rock looking out over the basin. At eye level with the deer, visibility had been zero, but from up here I could look right down into the dense alders and see anything that moved. For 2 hours I watched the basin like an eagle on a perch and saw nothing, but about 3 p.m. I could see limbs swaying in a clump of alders and through binoculars made out the back and antlers of a good buck. Another was feeding nearby. I picked out the larger of the two, carefully marked his position, and sneaked off my cliff to stalk that deer.

It took an hour to get from the cliff to his position, and he'd laid down in the meantime. Patiently I slipped along the edge of the alders, positive he was close. I climbed onto a boulder to look around and the buck heard me and stood up. He'd been bedded just on the other side of the boulder. He took a couple of steps and stopped at 15 yards to look back, and I put an arrow down through his back into his chest. That was my best buck up to that time, which was cause for elation. But even more satisfying was the realization that here was a method — a plan — that would put me in the driver's seat virtually anywhere I hunted.

DEFINING "STALK"

Before going farther I probably should define stalk, at least from my point of view, because stalking and still-hunting often are confused. "Still-hunting" means you sneak along quietly, looking for deer. You might feel confident you're in good game country, but you don't know the whereabouts of any one particular animal. You're just looking as you move along.

In stalking, by contrast, you don't start sneaking until you've located an animal. That could be by sound, as in bugling for elk, but more commonly, as in deer hunting, you locate animals by spotting. In essence, stalking and still-hunting are done the same way, but with one major difference — in still-hunting you're sneaking blind, but in stalking you're sneaking toward a definite, known object, and that distinction places the methods in two different worlds. Knowing the exact location of a deer before you start sneaking comes as close to guaranteed hunting as you'll find.

WHY SPOT-AND-STALK HUNTING?

NUMBERS. This method has several things going for it and sheer numbers is one. Spotting is the best way to see lots of deer. With high-power optics, you can look over a large expanse of country from one

I spotted this buck while looking straight down from a cliff into a dense alder patch. This experience proved to me that stalking would work not only in open country, but just about anywhere.

point, and because you're far beyond the sensory range of a deer's eyes, nose and ears, the animals carry on in a normal lifestyle, feeding in the open, bedding where they're easy to see, totally unaffected by the presence of man. They don't try to hide or sneak, because they don't know they're being watched.

And don't think for a minute that mule deer won't hide. One day I was walking across a sagebrush flat and crunched a piece of sage. In a low swale to my left, two deer peeked quickly my way and then ducked out of sight. Without question they saw me, and I expected to see them boil from the far side of the swale any moment. But after 5 minutes they hadn't showed so I slipped toward them, watching the brush ahead. Not 50 yards away I spotted the tips of antlers in the sage. When these deer saw me they hadn't run; they'd instantly dropped to the ground to hide. I was lucky to see them, and I could just as well have walked right by them.

Another time, as I watched from a cliff, two hunters were walking across a plateau, and at the same time a big buck, apparently spooked by another hunter, was running up from a canyon below. If the buck continued on course, he would run right in front of the two hunters on the plateau, so I sat tight to watch the fireworks.

But just before he broke over the top, the deer stopped suddenly — he must have smelled the hunters — and backed away below a small rim. He crept toward the men like a slinking cat and peeped over the rim to watch. He stood motionless for 10 minutes as the hunters walked within 30 yards. When they were 100 yards past, he snuck away and then took off fast. The last I saw of that buck, he was high-tailing over a ridge a mile

From a distance you can spot undisturbed deer, which gives you the biggest advantage you can have in bowhunting. If you watch this buck from far away until he moves into a stalkable position, you're virtually guaranteed to get a shot.

south. The two men never saw him. Undoubtedly this happens commonly, and hunters on foot who complain of seeing no deer have probably walked by more than they've seen.

When deer don't know you're around, they don't hide and as a result they're easy to spot. During an average day of deer hunting I expect to see anywhere from a dozen to three-dozen bucks. One morning in eastern Oregon my wife Laura and I sat on a cliff and from that one spot counted 50 bucks scattered across the sagebrush before us. Several times, I've spotted more than 100 in a day, and on my most incredible day I counted 155 bucks (that's bucks, not deer).

Even in forest country you can spot more deer than you would believe existed there. Frustrated by attempts at still-hunting for whitetails in northern Idaho, I decided to back off and try spotting across small draws just like in mule deer hunting except on a smaller scale. For the next four days I saw between 15 and 30 whitetail bucks a day. I wrote an article about that hunt for OUTDOOR LIFE magazine, and a guy from Pennsylvania wrote to me and called me a liar because he'd hunted whitetails all his life and had never seen that many in a season. He just didn't believe it could be true. I politely informed him he'd been hunting the wrong place, but I should have added he'd been using the wrong method. You might get close shots hunting from a tree stand as he'd been doing, but if you want to see lots of deer, you spot them from long range.

HUNTABLE DEER. Unfortunately, success isn't necessarily proportionate to the number of deer you see. The KINDS of deer you see is more important; those deer must be HUNTABLE. To be of any value, deer must be undisturbed and unaware, and once you've "choused" a buck, as they say in Arizona, you may never get another chance at him. A suspicious buck will manipulate you like a puppet, so the biggest advantage you can have over any deer is to see it before it sees you. That's the beauty of spotting, because you can see hundreds of deer without alerting them, and when you've spotted the one you want, you become the puppeteer.

That makes spotting and stalking the closest thing to a sure bet in the hunting world. I've never been crazy about hunting from a stand or still-hunting because these demand unending patience. You might argue that they don't require any more patience than sitting on a cliff for 3 hours, staring through a spotting scope, and that's true to some degree. However, in stand and still-hunting you never quite know where the deer are. In essence you're hunting blind. You're hunting intuitively, assuming deer are present based on sign, but you never know for sure. Hunting a "possible" buck demands too much patience for me.

Granted, in spotting it may take you a while to find a buck, and definitely — as we'll see in later chapters — stalking demands patience and control, but the fact is, when you go after a buck you've already spotted, you've eliminated a lot of guesswork. You know for sure you don't labor in vain. It's almost a sure thing.

I consider spotting and stalking a non-polluting approach to hunting. You can plant yourself on a cliff like this and watch deer from a distance so they never know you're around. Until it's too late.

NON-POLLUTING. One time a friend and I hunted a mountain basin together, and after a couple of days we'd worked over every deer that lived there. We were about to pack up and leave when we saw three deer way at the top of a ridge.

"Let's get after them," my friend said. "No sense in leaving those undisturbed."

For continued good hunting there is EVERY reason to leave them undisturbed. If you've ever hunting during a rifle season you know what happens after opening day. Deer vanish. Evaporate. Whether they get pushed into isolated refuge pockets or just move only at night is questionable, but one thing is for sure. They get scarce. The same thing can happen during bow seasons. If you kick them around, deer either disappear or get so spooky you can't move without putting something to flight.

Ron Granneman, a bowhunter who killed bull elk every one of his first 15 years of bowhunting, addressed this issue in relation to elk. Granneman said he liked to locate animals by bugling — opposed to still-hunting, tracking or taking a stand — because he could locate bulls at long range. He ghosts around the perimeter of prime areas, sticking to high ridges and trails, and bugling. He stays at long range until he hears a bull. Once he's located an animal, he moves in for a shot only when conditions are right. As soon as he enters the core area he knows he could spook elk, so he stays out until wind and weather are just right. He figures once he's disturbed those elk, not only might he run them out of the country, but even if he can find them again, they'll be twice as wary and difficult to bugle in.

The same principle applies to deer hunting. With an aggressive, let's-go-get-'em attitude, you'll have deer running everywhere, which can be exciting for a moment, but pretty soon those animals will disappear like water vapor under a hot sun, and you'll have to search for fresh animals.

With a cautious approach, you can sustain good hunting in one small area for many days, and that's the beauty of long range spotting. You're strictly an unseen observer. You can ghost around the edges of a hotbed, totally undetected while penetrating bedding and feeding areas with your eyes. In that small mountain basin mentioned above, my aggressive friend and I kicked out — or sent into hiding — virtually every deer within one day, and then we had to move on to find more game. In contrast I've hunted that same basin on my own for a week straight, and by staying at the edges, penetrating only with my eyes, and moving on deer only when conditions were right, I've hunted the same big bucks there day after day.

This point can't be overstressed. Do everything possible to avoid polluting an area. Move so your scent doesn't blow into the central area, and stay at the fringes so deer don't see or hear you. With that approach, you can hunt one prime canyon, or focus on hunting one particular buck, for a week or more and when the time is right, you can strike with assurance.

SELECTIVE HUNTING. A couple of years ago, Browning put on a hunt for some outdoor writers. Six of us participated on a ranch with lots of deer in northeastern Utah. Some Browning employees, along with guides at the ranch, ran the hunt, and they basically had all the bowhunters spread out and work up through canyons with the idea that we'd push deer back and forth to each other. In all fairness, it was a workable plan because deer were so plentiful that sooner or later we had to get some shooting.

Somehow, though, that didn't appeal to me, partly because I like to hunt alone, one-on-one, but also because it gave little opportunity for a trophy buck. It was strictly non-selective hunting, and we pretty much had to take what came along.

At the risk of appearing snobbish, I begged off one day and snuck off to do some spotting alone. Late that night I returned with a 3-point buck. It was no monster, but at the end of the four-day hunt, it won big-buck honors. The other five deer killed were forked horns. My hunting and shooting ability did not make the difference; my method did. When you still-hunt, take a stand, or drive deer, you have no assurance of seeing big bucks unless you've scouted intensively and know the routine of a particular deer. In spotting you can look over lots of deer in a short period of time, and you waste no time or energy stalking until you see the buck you want. It's selective hunting at its best, ideal for trophy hunting.

LAZY MAN'S WAY. On the subject of wasting time and energy, spotting and stalking can save you countless hours and miles of futile walking. Early in my bowhunting career, many hunters told me about catching bucks bedded under rimrocks, so following up on their advice, I snuck along desert rims for miles, peering over, trying to find a buck bedded there. My records show I walked well over 100 miles, yet not once did I ever spot a buck below a cliff, even though lots of beds indicated the presence of deer at one time or another.

One day I said to heck with walking and sat on a peak overlooking a broad flat that broke into a series of rimrocks. About mid-morning three bucks walked purposefully across the flat and dropped out of sight into the rims. I waited an hour for them to settle in, walked over to where they'd disappeared and immediately spotted one of the bucks bedded at the base of a cliff. I nailed him with an arrow at 40 yards. Walking and looking for deer is an exercise in futility, and just as I did in that case, you'll save yourself many fruitless miles by parking your rear end in one place and letting your eyes do the walking.

SIMPLICITY. One day I was walking across a sage flat in northern Nevada, where the stunted sagebrush scarcely reached as high as my ankles, and the nearest trees, a sparse clump of junipers, huddled in a draw a mile to the south. My footsteps crunched on the dry grass and scab rocks like a spoon mashing Rice Krispies, and the wind seethed with nagging ferocity. Frankly, I was loving every minute of it.

Maybe the reason was simplicity. Hunting there involved only placing one foot in front of the other and keeping my eyes open. Indeed open-country hunting requires skill, particularly in the form of game-spotting and physical control, but little more than good legs and the ability to use binoculars will put you in business. It doesn't demand a doctorate in deer behavior.

Dozens of books and thousands of magazine articles on whitetail hunting emphasize the need for scouting, study, knowledge of your quarry, ability to read sign, and so forth. You not only have to know a scrape when you see one, but you have to distinguish among primary scrapes, secondary scrapes, old scrapes, new scrapes, and you have to read tracks and urine sprays to know which way a buck was heading when he made the scrape, and if you're really sharp you'll know how to make mock scrapes, how to rattle, grunt and cough. Good grief. Whitetail lore gets so complicated it boggles my mind.

Some forms of mule deer hunting also require intense knowledge of your quarry. Dave Snyder, a Nevada bowhunter, has killed some of the finest western bucks ever taken by bowhunters, and Snyder hunts primarily from stands. Far be it for me to argue with the success of his method. It works.

Cal Coziah, who possibly has taken more trophy mule deer than any other bowhunter, is another legend in western bowhunting circles. Coziah's philosophy and methods differ from mine in some respects. He often uses his knowledge of terrain and an animal's movements to plan an ambush, or he stalks bucks, sight unseen, in heavy cover. Again, I'm not one to question the obvious effectiveness of his ways.

One thing these hunters' methods require, however, is the need for

In essence, scouting and hunting become the same thing in open country. Larry Jones and I spotted 10 bucks within our first minute in this country, and Larry killed this buck the second day there. That's the easy approach to hunting.

knowledge of the animals you're hunting. You must scout. I don't question the feasibility or the wisdom of that approach, and when time permits, I scout extensively to learn new country and the animals that live there. It's just that if you only get a week's vacation and must drive 1,000 miles to your hunting area, getting the needed knowledge quick enough to do any good can be tough. You don't have time to scout well.

That's where spotting and stalking comes into its own. This approach basically eliminates the need for scouting and reading of sign — all the technical stuff that goes with other forms of hunting. In open country, hunting and scouting are one and the same thing; you simply look for deer. You can hit a new area one day and be stalking bucks the next. One year my friend Larry Jones and I drove into a totally new mountain range. We'd done our homework by phone and on maps so we knew this place was good, but we'd never laid eyes on these mountains before. We drove to the top of a narrow ridge, parked the car, set up a spotting scope, and within a minute we'd spotted a group of 10 bucks lying in sparse aspens. We were in business, ready to stalk. Larry killed a buck the next day. Show me a simpler way to hunt.

EASY HUNTING

One time I wrote a magazine article on spot-and-stalk hunting. The editor eliminated my original title, and replaced it with: "If you can stalk desert mule deer, you can call yourself a hunter." That title implies that spotting and stalking can be really tough, the ultimate task in hunting, a view that contradicts the very point I was trying to make — that spotting and stalking is the EASY way to bowhunt for deer.

Indeed stalking can be a challenge, and no form of hunting will give you more thrill than creeping within spitting distance of an unsuspecting bucks, but the fact is, anybody can hunt this way.   I'm living proof of that. In the 7th grade I got cut from the basketball team — only five guys turned out — and I still stumble over cracks in the sidewalk. I'm hardly athletic, and my eyes are nothing to brag about either. Yet I can spot deer and get within bow range. Guaranteed. If I can do it, you can do it. It is, without question in my mind, the easiest and surest way to bowhunt for western bucks.

CHAPTER 3

OPTICS FOR SPOTTING

Binoculars and scopes form the core of the open-country hunting system. You have to be equipped right to kill anything, and without question, high-power optics are the most valuable equipment you'll ever buy, so don't take this seemingly dry aspect of hunting lightly.

MAGNIFICATION. With binoculars you can see game you'd never see with the naked eye, and you can size up trophy qualities of the deer you do see. Some hunters make extravagant claims for the eyesight of mule deer, but I can't go along with most of them. I seriously doubt that mule deer have eyes any better than the average person's. I've walked in plain sight of many deer no more than a half-mile away, and they've paid no attention. An antelope would spot you instantly at that distance, and I think elk would, too.

Still, deer are far from blind, and because they're familiar with every bush in their country and are very alert, they'll instantly notice anything out of place — namely you — so you want to do everything possible to get the upper hand. Assuming deer have eyes equal to yours, then your eyes, looking through 7x binoculars, are seven times as strong as a deer's. That gives you an immeasurable advantage. With binoculars you can sit far away and spot deer that will never know you're around, and that's THE basis for good hunting. If that link is weak, your entire hunting chain is weak.

BRIGHTNESS. Magnification may be most important, but brightness ranks a close second. Animals are classified according to their activity patterns. Deer are neither nocturnal (night) nor diurnal (day). Rather they're

At close range, binoculars have a shallow depth of field, which makes detail in the plane of focus stand out clearly and helps you spot deer in heavy cover. Blurred brush in front of and behind this doe isolates her and makes her easy to see.

crepuscular, which means they're most active during the grey light of dusk and dawn. As a result, you'll spot by far the most deer during the half-light of early morning and late evening. Some binoculars have the ability to gather light and actually brighten a scene, and that's a valuable asset for spotting deer. On the average I'd say good binoculars will lengthen your effective spotting time by at least a half hour at each end of the day.

DEPTH OF FIELD. It's often assumed that binoculars are meant only for long-distance spotting, but they're just as priceless at close range. As we'll see later, the ability to spot deer close plays a big part in stalking, and binoculars are the secret. At close range the depth-of-field of binoculars is very shallow, which in essence isolates detail. With binoculars, you can pick out an antler tine or an eyeball among a maze of branches that you'd never notice with your bare eyes.

One time I watched a buck walk into a clump of juniper trees. Since he never came out, I assumed he'd bedded there and went after him. The only problem was that the junipers were so thick they formed a solid curtain of twigs and needles. Where was the deer, and how would I ever spot him?

Looking through binoculars into the maze of branches, I dialed the focus knob back and forth to bring detail in different planes into focus. After 10 minutes of that, a square inch of gray suddenly caught my eye. It didn't look like part of an animal, but it didn't look like twigs or rocks either. I stared through the binoculars for several minutes when something moved above it. It was the buck all right. He was shaking his head against the flies, and the gray patch I'd first spotted was his foreleg where it met the ground. The shallow field of my binoculars at that close range, about 30 yards, isolated that gray patch from the confusing detail. Without the glasses I'd never have spotted that buck.

CHOOSING BINOCULARS

There are two basic kinds of binoculars — porro prism and roof prism. Porro prisms are the traditional humpback style, which are comparatively bulky and heavy. Roof prism binoculars have straight barrels, so for the same magnification, they're significantly slimmer and lighter.

Roof prisms, for comparable optical quality, are significantly more expensive. Al Akin, chief optical engineer for Bausch & Lomb, said that to get comparable optical quality, roof prism binoculars must be made much more precisely than porro prisms. The B&L 7x35 roof prisms, for example, cost almost twice as much as the equally sharp porro prisms, so you have to decide whether size and weight, or money, mean more to you. For years I used B&L Zephyr 7x35 porro prism binoculars and loved them, although at times the bulk got in the way a little. (Zephyrs are no longer made and have been replaced with the comparable Discoverers.) Recently I replaced those with the B&L 7x35 roof prisms. These are fantastic glasses, and I do appreciate the reduced size and weight.

SMALL SIZE. You can carry the size thing too far, however. In recent years, dozens of companies have come out with "mini" binoculars small enough to fit into a shirt pocket. The principle sounds great, but in fact it's self-defeating.

Brightness is the primary reason. Many of these binoculars are optically excellent, but they can't provide the brightness of full-size binoculars. If you hold your binoculars a foot or so from your face and look at the eye piece, you'll see a small point of light. That's called the exit pupil. In order for binoculars to deliver maximum brightness, the exit pupil must be as large as the pupil in your eye. Al Akin said the pupils in your eyes will dilate to a maximum of about 5 millimeters in dim light, so the exit pupil in your binoculars must be as large to give maximum brightness.

To figure exit-pupil size, simply divide the magnification into the size of the objective lens. (The first number in a binocular rating is the power, and the second is the size of the objective — front — lens.) For example, if you have 7x35 binoculars, you divide 7 into 35 and come up with 5. In other words, the exit pupil size is 5 millimeters, which is the size of your fully dilated eye and will give you excellent brightness.

That's where the rub comes in on the lightweight, compact binoculars. One popular size is the 8x20. That configuration sounds great — high magnification, small size — but when you divide 20 (objective lens size) by 8 (magnification) you come up with an exit pupil size of 2.5 millimeters, which is half the size of the pupil in your eye. As a result, these binoculars reduce the amount of light entering your eye and actually can make a scene look darker rather than brighter. One year I bought 8x20 binoculars because the light weight and small size seemed ideal for backpacking. I hunted a half-day with them, and even in good midday light the glasses seemed to make the country look dark. I was so disappointed I hiked several miles back to my truck to trade them for my heavier 7x35 Zephyrs. Compacts may be okay for detail checking from a stand or other casual uses, but for serious hunting, full-size glasses are the only choice.

BIG BINOCULARS. You can carry large size too far, too. For example, it would seem the 7x50 binocular would be ideal because the exit pupil measures 7.1 millimeters. Al Akin said the increased size of the exit pupil has value only if it's no larger than the size of the dilated pupils in your eyes. Since maximum pupil size is about 5 millimeters, your eyes aren't able to utilize all the extra light transmitted by the large exit pupil, so the apparent brightness of the 7x50 is not appreciably greater than that of the 7x35. It's probably not enough to make carrying the extra bulk and weight worthwhile.

BUY QUALITY. Cheap glasses can cause tremendous eye strain. In serious open-country hunting you may look through your binoculars 4 or 5 hours a day, so you want the marriage between you and your optics to be right. My first couple of years of bowhunting, I borrowed cheap discount-store binoculars to save money. I could see well-enough with them, but after an hour of glassing I'd get dizzy and stagger around like a drunk, and after a full-day's use those things gave me a headache that

Both pairs of 7X35 Bausch & Lomb binoculars shown here are optically comparable, but the roof prisms glasses at left are somewhat smaller and lighter in weight than the porro prisms. The roof prisms also cost more. You have to decide whether economy of size or money is more important to you.

lasted the entire hunt. I couldn't take enough aspirin to get rid of the pain. So I got rid of the binoculars and invested in quality glasses and have never regretted it.

Good binoculars can brighten a scene and extend your spotting time at least a half-hour at each end of the day. Notice how much larger the exit pupil is on the 7X35 binoculars on the bottom than on the 8X20s on top. The larger exit pupil means much brighter glasses.

One problem with cheap glasses is poor alignment, which means the lenses actually point in different directions. Your eyes attempt to pull the images together, and the muscles that control your eyes go bananas.

The poor optical quality of cheap binoculars strains your eyes, too. Al Akin said that the lenses of good binoculars are polished to produce a perfectly clear image, but in cheap glasses, specifications aren't nearly as precise. Your eyes try to draw the view into focus, and this continuous attempt to do the impossible produces burning eyes and a splitting headache.

Cheap binoculars generally aren't well constructed so you're liable to have mechanical troubles with them, and they'll commonly fog up inside, forcing you to wait for them to dry out before you can see anything, which can be more than a little aggravating when you think you've just spotted a monster buck. Because of close manufacturing tolerances, high-quality binoculars rarely if ever fog up. In short, good glasses are rugged and if treated half-way decently, will last forever.

On this last point, you can now buy binoculars that are waterproof and fogproof, and you also can get rubber armored binoculars. These are good features that you may want to consider. However, don't trade optical quality for the razzle-dazzle of flashy features. Some companies put a rubber coating around cheap binoculars and tout them as ideal for hunting, but down inside they're still cheap. Other companies, such as Zeiss and Bausch & Lomb, armor coat some of their best optics. You'll have to decide whether the extra weight of the rubber is worth the added protection. For wet-country hunting, you'll want to consider fully waterproof glasses, but for most open-country desert hunting, they aren't necessary. During the occasional desert rainstorm, I just slip my binoculars inside my shirt to keep them dry.

JUDGING QUALITY. With a couple of quick tests, you can roughly gauge the quality of binoculars in a store. Ken Morris, an optical engineer for Bushnell, said the prisms in cheap glasses are made with inexpensive glass that doesn't transmit all incoming light, and in these the exit pupil appears squarish. Prism glass in good binoculars transmits all incoming light to the eye, and in these the exit pupil is perfectly round.

Also, when you look through cheap binoculars, the center of the image may appear sharp, but toward the edges it will be blurred. In good glasses, the image is sharp to the very edges. Don't try to gauge this by looking through a store window, because the window will distort the image. Go outside where you can get a clear view.

You may be able to gauge quality by price, too. Morris said you can bank on binoculars over $300, and those in the $200 price range will be more than adequate. Many binoculars in the $100 range are acceptable for general hunting, but they may not have the precise optical quality or rugged dependability you need for serious hunting. When you get down to the $50 range, you're buying nothing but headaches.

MAGNIFICATION. For all-around use, I consider 7x or 8x binoculars the best choice. Magnification affects not only image size, but also field-of-view (the amount of area you can see at one time), relative brightness and stability. It would seem the higher the magnification, the better the binoculars, but as in all good things, the law of diminishing returns applies, and as you gain in magnification, you lose in other areas.

We've already discussed brightness above. The higher the power the larger the objective lens must be to retain an acceptable level of brightness, and the larger the binoculars will be. You have to decide whether the added magnification justifies the larger size and weight.

Also, the higher the magnification, generally the narrower the field of view. A narrow field of view is not a problem if you're glassing out to a mile or more in expansive desert, but if you're hunting confined country where visiblity may be no more than 100 yards to a quarter-mile, you might find the narrow field-of-view more restrictive than you'd like.

A 10x binocular magnifies not only distant objects 10 times, which is good, but it also magnifies movement of the binoculars 10 times, which can be bad. Most people, providing their hands are fairly steady, can hand hold binoculars from 6x to 8x, but glasses in the 9x and 10x range are hard to hand hold, especially if you're winded or excited from hard hunting. If you plan to hunt primarily in the open desert and prairies where visibility is nearly unlimited, you'll love 9x and 10x glasses. But for all around hunting, which includes closer-range spotting in timbered or broken country, you'll probably find 7x or 8x more versatile.

OPTICS COMBINATION. If I could choose only one piece of optical equipment for all hunting, I'd probably pick a high-quality 8x or 9x binocular. However, binoculars alone aren't adequate for all situations, so I generally use a combination. My long-time favorite system consists of Bausch & Lomb's 7x35 roof prism binoculars along with a Bushnell Stalker 20x scope. That combination has proved adequate for all situations. With binoculars like that you can spot deer out to a mile or so, and with the scope you can go right on out to 2 or 3 miles. Just as important, with the scope you can judge antlers accurately. Using only binoculars, you scarcely can see antlers on a big buck a mile away, but with the scope you can estimate antler size accurately.

CHOOSING A SCOPE

A variable-power scope, say from 15x to 60x, might seem ideal, but in buying a zoom scope you're paying for something you rarely can use. In desert and prairie country, heat waves shimmer from the ground even on cool days, and these distort the view so badly that you can see nothing at higher magnification. I've found that anything stronger than 30x is wasted in desert hunting.

For the money you get a better buy with a fixed-power scope. Twenty power has proved best all-around for me, although you could get by with 25x. Fifteen power isn't quite strong enough, in my opinion. Bushnell now makes the Stalker with a zoom range of 10x to 30x and this may be the best choice of all. It will cover just about every situation.

The Stalker is also light in weight, which makes it ideal for off-road hunting. I love the Stalker scope because it weighs less than 8 ounces and fits neatly into my day pack. For that reason I'll carry it to backcountry places when I'd leave a heavier scope in camp. Redfield makes an even smaller 30x scope with a mirror lens. In terms of size and weight it's ideal for backcountry hunting, but the mirror lens system is not as sharp as the standard lens system, and I wouldn't want to rely on this scope for critical, long-range spotting. If you hunt strictly from your vehicle or on horseback where size and weight pose no obstacle, then the high-optical quality of scopes such as Bushnell's Spacemaster or Trophy can be a great asset.

PUTTING OPTICS TO USE

Binoculars — or any optical equipment for that matter — are useless unless you use them. Okay, so that sounds obvious, but it never ceases to amaze me how many hunters carry their binoculars in a case or in their daypacks to keep them clean. Hunting with guys like that can drive you nuts because you always have to stop and wait as they dig out their glasses, and then take off the lens caps, and then find their special tissue to wipe the lenses clean. By the time they get ready to spot, the deer have all bedded for the day or been shot by some other hunter.

KEEP THEM HANDY. You have to be ready all the time to spot lots of game, and you have to be looking constantly. If getting out your binoculars is a hassle, you just won't bother most of the time, and you won't see half the deer you should see. Hunting equipment was made to be used, so keep it handy where it can do its job.

You can stuff small binoculars into your shirt pocket and get at them easily, but if you really want your glasses handy, hang them around your neck. To keep them from swinging, tie a piece of elastic to the binoculars and stretch that around your back. The elastic holds the glasses secure against your chest, but it stretches enough so you can pull them quickly to your eyes. One hunter told me he holds his binoculars against his chest with a Velcro tab, and my friend Larry Jones has his wife sew a big pocket right on the chest of his shirt so he can slip the glasses into it to take the weight off his neck.

Al Akin, who has spent his life working with optical equipment, says lens caps are worthless, because they only get in the way when you're hunting. I agree. Here again, if you have to fumble with the caps every time you want to check out a deer, you'll just say to heck with it half the time.

CLEANING LENSES. All high-quality optics have coated glass, which is scratch resistant, so a little dirt on the lenses won't hurt anything. The chief danger, Akin said, is dry dust because it's abrasive, so blow away as much dust as possible before wiping the lenses. If possible, use soft lens tissue, and moisten it before you rub it on the lenses. If you don't have tissue handy, a soft T-shirt is okay as long as you moisten it before wiping away dust.

Incidentally, a hard knock will throw even the best binoculars out of alignment. Never take binoculars apart, for any reason, to repair them yourself. You'll never get the alignment right again. That requires specialized equipment, so always return them to the manufacturer or to a specialized repair service.

HOLD THEM STEADY. The best optics in the world will do you little good if they're not used right, and above all they must be steady. Any scope over 15x must be supported on a padded rest or held on a tripod. In tall grass or other cover where my small tripod isn't high enough, I can set the tripod-and-scope combination on my knee and see well enough to evaluate a deer, but for most spotting with a scope, you have to mount the scope on a tripod and set in on the ground or on a rock to get the full value.

The same can be said for binoculars. Even with 7x glasses, you see best if you set them on a tripod or other solid support. If you don't believe me, try it. You'll see!

Realistically, though, you probably won't carry a tripod around everywhere you go — at least I won't — but you can still hold your glasses steady. It may be okay to stand and throw the glasses to your eyes to check a quick detail, but for serious spotting, that won't get it. Sit down to glass. If you can support your glasses on a limb or rock, so much the better. If you can't find convenient support, sit with your knees drawn up. Rest your elbows on your knees, and then wrap your hands around the binoculars and brace your fingers against your forehead. In this position you can hold the glasses steady.

USING A SCOPE. With a scope you look with only one eye, so you can suffer terrible eye strain. I think the real problem is muscle strain from squinting the eye that's not looking through the scope. To ease tension, don't squint that eye but rather cover it with your hand. With both eyes wide open, your face can relax and you won't get the headaches you do when you close one eye.

For any kind of effective spotting, you have to mount your scope on a tripod. To be comfortable, use a tripod with extendable legs so you can sit in a comfortable position as you glass. If you have to crouch over or lie down, an hour's glassing will make you feel like you've been in a wrestling match.

Ideally all optics should be supported by a tripod, but that's not always feasible. As an alternative, support your elbows on your knees and brace your hands against your forehead, and you'll have steady support.

ANOTHER SYSTEM

Duwane Adams, a trophy hunter and outfitter in Arizona, doesn't use a spotting scope, and he uses small binoculars only for close-range checking during a stalk. For general spotting he uses Zeiss' 15x60 binoculars. These binoculars are big and heavy, but they're incredibly sharp and bright. Adams prefers them over a spotting scope because he can use both eyes all the time.

"I started out using a scope just like everybody else," Adams said. "But squinting through that thing all day was more than I could take. With these binoculars, I'm still spotting game when the guys with the scopes are rubbing their burning eyes and taking aspirin for a headache."

He emphasizes that 15x binoculars must be absolutely motionless to be of any value. For that reason he always mounts them on a tripod. He also figures you have to be comfortable and relaxed to spot game all day, so he uses a folding tripod that, when extended, puts the binoculars right at eye level when he's sitting. He also carries a small pad to sit on to keep his rear end dry and free of cactus spines. He carries all of this in a weather-proof bag tied on a lightweight packframe.

To find game, he sits on a point overlooking a broad expanse of mule deer or Coues whitetail country, and he sets his binoculars on the tripod right at eye level. When he looks through those stationary binoculars, it's just like watching for deer through a 15x picture window, and he can pick up the slightest movement and detail on distant hillsides. Adams hunts strictly by spotting, and his success as a trophy hunter verifies the value of his system. He frequently spots Coues whitetails, which are about half the size of mule deer, as far as 4 miles away.

If you're really serious about game spotting, consider Adams' system. He has all of his guides converted, mainly because when it came to spotting game, they just couldn't compete with him any other way. The chief drawbacks are the price of the binoculars — in the $1,000 range — and the heavy weight of the glasses. I'd hate to pack those 3-pound glasses on a long backpacking trip.

Whatever method you choose, get the best optics you can afford and learn to use them. If you skimp on eye power, you'll skimp on success. You'll see!

CHAPTER 4

SPOTTING

The biggest change in my deer hunting fortunes came when I learned it really was possible to spot deer before they saw me. Oh, I'd tried, but still it seemed that every time I saw a buck he was always barreling the other way, sending up clouds of dust with every bound.

During one of my first couple of years of bowhunting, Rod Schooler, an experienced desert hunter, told me he'd seen 18 bucks out feeding one day. Secretly I said, "Baloney!" because I'd covered every square inch of that same country and hadn't seen 18 bucks in a week, let alone one day, and I'd certainly never seen them out feeding and vulnerable. As much to prove him wrong as to learn, I talked him into taking me along one morning.

Rod drove out a rocky desert trail, parked his truck and set a spotting scope right on the hood. "That's his first mistake," I thought. "You can't spot deer from a road. You've got to hoof it!"

A couple of minutes later, Rod said, "Bingo. He's in that draw at the far end of the flat."

"Let me see. Let me see!" I said, wondering how he could spot a deer that far away. It had to be more than a mile. I looked through the spotting scope and saw a blur of heat waves. "I don't see him."

Rod looked again. "He's right in the middle of the scope."

I looked again. "You're kidding. I don't see any deer."

Rod looked again. "Right in the middle."

I strained through the scope, desperately trying to see a deer to avoid looking like a complete fool. Finally I made out some branches moving in the shimmering heat waves. No, those were antlers. "Hey, there's a deer in here. It's a buck!" After that Rod couldn't tear me away. I had to look. This was a new sight, a buck feeding out in the open. Not spooked. Man, what a sight!

From that same point, Rod spotted another buck, and later he pointed out three more bucks bedded in high sage on the side of a rolling hill. Those bucks either didn't know we were there, or at that distance they didn't care. Looking through the scope was like sitting right there beside those deer as they carried on without a care. On my own, I wouldn't have seen any of them, or at the least they would have been spooked and running. This revelation changed my hunting life. Since that day many years ago, I've glassed hundreds, if not thousands, of deer, and these experiences over the years have convinced me that on that one day I discovered the secret to all good deer hunting. Spotting.

LOCATION

Another experience during that same year taught me an important lesson in spotting — that you have to look in the right places to see deer. This lesson came from Dan Herrig, a graduate student who'd spent all summer in the desert studying antelope and deer. One morning Herrig and I were driving along a winding gravel road among open sage knobs when Herrig suddenly hit the breaks and slid to a halt.

"There's a buck up there in that snowbrush," he said, pointing to the top of a hill a half-mile away. I had to scan several minutes with binoculars to see that buck. We continued on down the road and twice more he spotted bucks out feeding, and each time I had to stop and use the binoculars to see them.

Over the years I've asked myself why he spotted so many animals that totally escaped me. I'm convinced it wasn't because his eyes were better than mine; it was because he knew where to look. While I gawked around aimlessly, scanning at all the pretty spots where the willows and aspen trees grew, Herrig's eyes probed prime feeding pockets and resting areas favored by bucks at that time of year. Through experience he'd learned that bucks like certain kinds of country, and his eyes naturally concentrated on those places.

You often read that the secret to spotting game is looking for horizontal lines or twitching ears and those tips are valid, but I'm convinced WHERE you look is far more important than HOW you look. If you put yourself in a good spot, you can be half blind and still spot lots of game.

THE POCKET PRINCIPLE

Lesson No. 1 in game spotting reads: All deer country is not created equal.

Within any good range, some pockets will hold bunches of deer and the

I rank location as the most important single aspect of deer spotting. If you look in the right spot you can't help but see lots of bucks, but you have to find just the right pocket. That's why you're wise to look around and get an overview of your country before you settle into one spot to hunt.

rest of the country will be virtually empty. That's why I think it's important to move around to get an overview of your hunting country before you settle in to hunt one spot. If you find a buck or two in one basin and stick right there without looking farther, you could be settling for mediocre hunting when you could enjoy fantastic action just over the next ridge.

It all boils down to what I call the pocket principle. Deer, and especially bucks, congregate in particular spots, and for best hunting you have to find those places. You may look over a lot of country and see virtually nothing, even though it looks ideal, and then suddenly you'll discover a concentration of bucks you can't believe.

That happened to me in an Oregon desert range. I drove in specifically to hunt a huge basin filled with aspen trees and lush pockets of sage, bitterbrush and other deer delicacies, a fine piece of deer country. In two days I saw only two bucks and assorted does. Where could all the deer be? This country had to hold more animals than that.

Determined to find them, I took off cross country, and from every high cliff and hilltop spent an hour or more staring through binoculars, looking for deer. I'd hiked a good 5 miles and looked over several empty basins before I finally hit the jackpot. More than 30 bucks had concentrated in one open, treeless canyon. The country wasn't nearly as good looking for deer as the aspen bowl, but deer were thick. The next two days held some of the finest deer hunting I've ever experienced, all because I persisted and kept moving and looking to find the prime pocket.

In that case I suspect the deer had been pushed from the aspen bowl by hunters — there was evidence of several camps — and had probably concentrated in that desolate, isolated canyon because nobody had disturbed them there, but deer will congregate in pockets for other reasons. Water is one. During drought years I've found bucks as thick as flies at the highest elevations around water sources, but during rainy years they've been scattered far and wide out across the desert. The quality of feed also can affect distribution.

These variables can change from year to year so never make any assumptions about where you'll find deer. Even in country you've hunted for years, plan to look around before you settle on a definite plan, because bucks may not be concentrated in the same places they were previous years.

FOR BUCKS ONLY. Within any given mule deer range, you'll often find bucks and does living separately during summer bow seasons. In general you'll find bucks living at the highest, most inhospitable, and most open locations. The fact that bucks gravitate toward open country makes them particularly susceptible to spotting and stalking. That's not to say you won't find bucks living in aspens and oak brush and heavy timber, because you will. Habitat varies so much from region to region, it's hard to generalize, but I'll try anyway.

In the Great Basin deserts I started out hunting aspen groves and bottomlands, assuming any deer in his right mind would favor the lushest country where the living was easy. Definitely lots of deer lived there, but it soon became obvious 90 percent of them were does and fawns. A few smaller bucks hung around these places, but rarely any mature bucks.

Then I started roaming the open sage flats, rimrocks, steep canyons and other inhospitable places where the wind blew and the sun blazed with ceaseless intensity, and that's where the bucks showed up. At first I assumed they'd been harassed by hunters in the aspen groves and mahogany patches and were forced to dwell in unholy lands to escape people. To some degree I'm sure that's true, but in recent years I've returned to my hunting grounds to photograph deer during mid-summer, well ahead of hunting seasons when nobody was around, and I've found bucks living in the same open, desolate places.

That observation doesn't apply just to deserts and prairies. In Oregon's Wallowa Mountains there's a place we call "The Moon" because it's nothing but sand and granite rock. Why deer would live up there is beyond me, because it seems like the most unwholesome place in the entire mountain range. A few clumps of grass and some lupines struggle for survival in cracks in the granite, but the feed could hardly be considered lush.

Yet deer tracks pock the entire area. One morning a friend and I watched five bucks cavort and chase each other for a half-hour up there, and another morning I saw four different bucks with antler spreads of 25 to 30 inches. You'd think those deer would head down into the timber to bed, but commonly I've seen them right up in the granite, lying in the sparse shade of lone, stunted pine trees. In most western states I've found bucks concentrated around similar alpine "deserts."

VELVET ANTLERS. Maybe bucks live in that sort of country, where they can see forever and feel the cool breezes, just because they like it. Maybe getting up high and looking down on the world makes them feel good, just as it makes most people feel good. But it probably goes deeper than that. As I said in Chapter 1, bucks apparently prefer open country over timber during summer to avoid banging up their soft antlers.

In late summer bucks such as the one I'm admiring here still have velvet on their antlers, and they'll stay in the open where brush and trees won't bang up their tender antlers. That's one reason you'll see lots of bucks during early seasons.

Of course, there's a corollary to that rule, and it's important to remember for successful spotting, too. When their antlers harden up about September 1, bucks will readily move into the brush and timber. Lee Kline, a very successful bowhunter from Colorado, said he thinks mule deer become different animals as soon as they shed their velvet, changing from animals of the high, wide and open above timberline to creatures of the aspen and oak brush. I think that's true and it should influence the places where you look for bucks.

I've had excellent spotting right on through September and into October, however, in the same places where I've seen lots of bucks in August. As long as the feed remains good and hunters aren't too numerous, bucks often will stay right where they spent the summer.

GENTLEMEN BUCKS. Soft antlers may be one reason bucks like open country, but their preference also may be a natural strategy for preservation of the species. Dave Pac, a deer biologist in Montana, said it's not an illusion that bucks tend to hang out in more desolate country than does. In essence, does with fawns need the abundant feed, water and shelter provided by lusher low country. In the scheme of species survival, their needs come first, and as a result bucks are forced to inhabit the less productive reaches of a given range.

This tendency for bucks to congregate in isolated pockets has spawned the term "buck pasture," and indeed such places do exist. In the bottomlands you'll find all kinds of does and fawns and small bucks, but when you start scratching around the open desert or badlands, you'll suddenly find a concentration of bucks in the most unlikely places. It's common to see bucks running in herds of a half-dozen animals, and in a good buck pasture you'll probably locate several such small groups. In others you might find one big herd. Commonly I've seen as many as two-dozen bucks in a herd, and up to as many as 80.

THE EXCEPTIONS. Primarily I've discussed late summer conditions, because that's when most general archery seasons take place. Of course, as the fall progresses, conditions will change. When bucks become hard horned, they'll be more eager to move into timber and cover, either to escape hunters or to look for better feed as early frosts burn the grass and shrubs at high elevations.

In November — January in the Southwest — deer go into rut and obviously then you'll find bucks and does together, and they may hang out in the same general areas on into winter. Winter weather becomes the great equalizer, and during harsh periods bucks and does are forced onto the same ranges. Even then, though, you'll most likely find the older bucks hanging out in pockets by themselves, away from the main herds.

PINPOINT SPOTTING

One August my friend Larry Jones and I sat on a cliff in central Utah, glassing a big basin. We'd seen enough deer there previous days to know it was an exceptional buck pasture, and before long we spotted a couple of deer bedded in an aspen grove.

"Why do you think those bucks are bedded there?" Larry said. He's the analytical type who's always trying to figure things out, and he was making a sincere attempt to analyze this situation.

"Probably because they're sleepy," I said. Larry gave me a dirty look and started throwing rocks at me. "Larry, shhh, you'll scare the deer. Quit. I'm sorry!"

Despite my smart aleck answer, I knew Larry was on the right track. Deer do prefer certain spots over others for bedding and feeding, and you'll see by far the most game if you learn to recognize those spots right off.

COOL PLACES. The advice Dan Herrig gave me years ago still holds up as reliable today. During early seasons, Herrig said, he concentrates his spotting efforts on north and east slopes where feed is most succulent and shade provides cool bedding sites.

Herrig's philosophy makes sense. Throughout the West, prevailing winds come from the south and west, so snow drifts on the north and east sides of ridges. Moisture from deep drifts lasts well into the summer, watering lush growths of shrubs and trees. On most north-facing pockets throughout western deserts and mountains, you'll see what biologists generally refer to as "mountain brush types," a combination of plum, chokecherry, various species of Ceanothus, and other green plants. Even in the most stark deserts, you'll find pockets of lush snowbrush clumped on sheltered, moist slopes, and you can bet most bucks will focus in on these green spots. As you glance at even distant, unfamiliar desert ranges, you'll notice shades of green on the north and east-facing slopes that mark the presence of succulent shrubs. With experience you'll know those mean "Deer!"

In a timberline setting of high, forested mountains, the green spots often take the form of willow or alder patches, or lush meadows surrounding spring areas. Even here the "green" principle applies — where lush greenery contrasts with surrounding dry brown, you'll most likely find a concentration of deer.

Some good deer country, however, doesn't have any green vegetation at all. Purple sage may just stretch for mile after monotonous mile, but still you'll find deer there. In some of my favorite hunting places, deer feed and bed right out in the middle of huge sage flats. In some cases the sage and bitterbrush where they feed is higher than the surrounding brush, but in many cases it all looks the same and I can't figure out why they pick one spot over another. Even on these seemingly featureless flats and plateaus, however, I find that bucks consistently use the same places, so if you spot deer in a particular place once, remember it well. Chances are you'll frequently spot bucks in the same spots.

That's particularly true in steep canyons where flat spots and shade are at a premium. Deer will bed under the same trees or cliffs day after day, year after year. These beds may be dug out several feet deep. When you discover traditional bedding sites, make note of them because chances are good you'll spot deer there time after time.

VANTAGE POINTS

Once you've found good deer country and have an idea of where to look, an additional important step is locating good places to spot from. I know a number of guys who hunt strictly by driving roads and glassing, and they won't leave their rigs until they've spotted a buck and watched him bed down. Actually that's not a bad way to hunt because deer will often ignore a vehicle when they'll run like crazy from a person on foot. Spotting from roads severely limits your potential, though, and you'll never see some of those hidden buck pastures all hunters dream about. Personally, I think the farther you hunt from roads, the better your hunting will be in the long run.

Regardless of whether you spot from your vehicle or on foot, you have to find good glassing points. I've said scouting doesn't play a big part in spot-and-stalk hunting because you scout as you hunt, but it does help to look around to find good glassing points.

GOOD VIEW. First you want to locate places where you can see an expanse of good deer country. In timbered canyons or alpine terrain, that might mean you'll be overlooking 5 acres of brush, but in desert or prairie it could mean viewing an open plateau 3 miles long or one entire side of a huge canyon.

That generally means picking the highest point possible. Not only does a high glassing position help you to see more country, but from above you can look down into brush to see deer you'd never see from their level or below.

UNSEEN. Look for places where you can get into position without being seen. If you have to walk in plain view of the deer you plan to hunt, you're defeating yourself before you start. Try to find places where you can just slip over a cliff or through a grove of trees and sit down, and try to approach spotting places with rocks, trees or other cover behind you. A cardinal sin is skylining yourself. If you've got a backdrop deer probably won't notice you at a quarter-mile, but if you're silhouetted on a skyline they'll catch you instantly at a mile or more.

THE SUN. To spot effectively, you must be looking away from the sun. Most commonly deer will feed and bed in shadows. If you're looking toward shadows with the sun in your face, the shadows will appear nearly black, and you'll be hard pressed to see animals there. It's best to spot with the sun directly behind you, or if that's not possible, at the least to the side. Obviously, you have to spot from different points in the evening than in the morning.

THE WIND. It's just as important to consider wind direction. When you're looking for deer a mile away, you might wonder what difference wind might make, but don't kid yourself. In open country, deer could very well smell you at that distance. One time Laura and I watched a bunch of deer bedded at the head of a canyon. Straight across it was a half-mile from our position to the deer. The wind was swirling, but the deer were so far that didn't seem like a problem. We'd sat there 10 minutes or so when they jumped up, sniffing the air and then trotted away. We were the only ones around, and we'd been sitting still out of sight for some time, so I'm sure they'd smelled us.

Another time I walked toward a glassing position and had to cross upwind of some deer. I'd seen them go into a draw out of sight where they couldn't see me, and they were so far away it seemed impossible they'd ever smell me, but about 20 seconds after I'd crossed upwind of them, they boiled out of that draw like bees from a hive. There was no doubt they'd smelled me. I later drove from my position to the draw where the deer had been, and the odometer showed it was three-quarters of a mile.

Try to figure out the wind patterns for a given area, and pick spotting positions accordingly. In most cases, a breeze will be drifting downhill early in the morning so you don't want to sit on a canyon rim and look for deer below you. Plant yourself on the far rim and look back into the side where you expect to see deer.

As you learn a piece of country, you'll adjust your spotting position to suit your needs. Duwane Adams, the outfitter in Arizona, said anytime he's hunting new country, he searches out the highest point or ridge he can find, and he spends his first day sitting right there, looking for game. He doesn't confine his efforts to nearby territory. With his 15x60 binoculars, he looks for deer as far away as 3 or 4 miles. The first day of looking gives him a good idea of where to find the most game. To put it another way, he scouts with his eyes. At the same time he looks for other good vantage points, and the next day, before daylight, he moves into a new glassing position, this time much closer to the animals, so that when he spots them the second day he'll be within stalking range.

TIME OF DAY

Location ranks as the most important aspect of deer spotting, but time of day runs a close second. Quite frankly, open-country deer are easy to spot if you look when the looking is easy. As we've already discussed, deer are most active in the grey light of dawn and dusk. At these times the animals venture into the open to feed, and when they're in the open, walking around, anybody who takes time to look can see them.

My first year of spotting, Laura and I set out with beginners' zeal. We started hiking from camp at 4 a.m. and arrived at a preselected spotting point at 5:30. At that time we couldn't even detect the slightest glow of sunrise so we snuggled together — one added benefit of taking your wife — until 6 o'clock when we could start to see. Within 10 minutes we'd spotted two 3-points, 2 forked horns and a doe. Those were the first deer we'd ever really "spotted" on our own, and we were ecstatic. We were hooked on early-morning spotting. Probably one reason we'd failed to see deer in previous seasons was that we'd never really got out early enough.

During his summers in the desert, Dan Herrig said he'd observed that as a common problem. "Most hunters are just heading out in the morning when they should be heading in, and they're coming back to camp in the afternoon when they should be heading out to hunt," Herrig said. "They just don't hunt early and late enough to see many deer."

VISIBLE DEER. For a couple of reasons, I think morning is by far the best time to spot deer. Under the cover of darkness, deer apparently feel secure out in the open with no concealment, and so during the night they disperse far from cover. Early in the morning just after daylight they're still out there where you can see them from miles away. As daylight comes, they start drifting toward bedding cover. Under some conditions — I'll talk more about those in a minute — deer will linger in the open until 10 a.m. or longer, but more often they'll disappear soon after sunrise, and if you're not out there early, you'll miss most of them.

One year the weather was particularly sweltering in August in the eastern Oregon desert. Just at daylight I watched a buck far out on a sagebrush plateau scrubbing the velvet off his antlers on a bush. He wandered around out there, feeding and fighting bushes for an hour or so. Right at 8 o'clock he deliberately turned and walked to a nearby rim and disappeared into a clump of junipers. I saw lots of bucks that year, but every day by 8 o'clock they stopped feeding abruptly and walked to shady canyons to bed. If I'd been slow in getting out, I'd have sworn there wasn't a deer in the country.

The same holds true under heavy hunting pressure. Deer seem to evaporate when they've been harassed by hunters, but the question is: Do they head for parts unknown, or do they just become nocturnal? Hart Mountain makes a good laboratory to study such things. Before the season you can go over there and see 30 bucks most any day, but after opening weekend of the bow season, those bucks vanish. We always assumed they bailed off into inaccessible canyons or disappeared into the vast expanses of desert, but I'm not sure that's true.

One year, after the season had been open several days, we discovered a buck bedded within 300 yards of the most crowded campground on the mountain. We'd never have seen that buck except that as we drove by he raised his head just high enough to peek at us over the sage and then dropped back down out of sight. We later pulled a sneak on him but blew it and chased him out of the country. Three days later two friends of mine caught him in exactly the same place. Apparently that buck had stuck with his home range, but he'd started feeding and moving at night, and I think that's a common pattern. If the deer seem to disappear, you may not need to look for them in new places; you just need to look for them earlier and later in the day.

TIME TO STALK. Morning presents ideal spotting for another reason.

As we'll see later, you need time to stalk. If you spot a buck in the morning, you often can watch him bed down and you've got all day to work on him. It's true that you can spot deer in the evening as they emerge from cover to feed, but often you won't see them until late afternoon. Stalking then becomes a race with night, and trying to stalk a feeding buck quickly is tough. It can be done, but not consistently. For the greatest hope, you want a lot of time to stalk a bedded deer, and morning spotting offers the surest chance for that.

Incidentally, spotting bucks as they feed in the morning is the way to locate bedded bucks. Definitely, as we'll see later, you can spot bucks after they're bedded, but the easy way is to locate them as they feed and watch them bed down.

NO POLLUTION. There's one more good reason for getting out early in the morning, and that is, again, to avoid spooking deer. If you casually stroll to your spotting position in daylight, you'll sooner or later get caught, but before daylight, you can get into position unseen.

I always try to organize my gear the night before so I can take off hiking early and get to my spotting position well before first light. Cliff Dewell, a California hunter who has taken a number of big sagebrush bucks, strongly emphasizes the need for getting into position unseen. He figures even a spooked coyote or any slight disturbance could hamper his chances at the buck he's after. Often, if it's a long way from camp to where he wants to hunt, he'll load his sleeping bag and a light shelter onto his packframe, hike to his hunting area and sleep there so he can start looking right at daylight.

Maybe this all sounds a little fanatical, and certainly it doesn't wash with every opinion. Cal Coziah, perhaps the West's most successful bowhunter, said he hates to get up early, and he almost makes a fetish of sleeping in. Again, no one will argue with his success, but don't be misled into thinking that's the way you'll kill bucks. Coziah often hunts them in their bedding areas, and he knows his country intimately so that he can tell you where he'll find bucks even before he leaves camp. He has proved it can be done, but if you're hunting new country and really want to see some deer, I'd suggest you get out early.

SPOTTING LATE

Now, to contradict myself, I'll say you often can spot deer all day long. That's one of the beauties of hunting by spotting. You can still spot up some action, even after everything has died for the day, if you have patience. Some hunters are ready to give up if they're not out there before the crack of dawn, but I wouldn't let that frustrate me. On a hunt sponsored by Browning in Utah, circumstances prevented our getting out early a couple of mornings, and one of the guys nearly worked up a heart attack because he thought we'd never see any deer. As it turned out the deer were relatively undisturbed and we had no problem spotting game most any time.

One morning Glenn Helgeland, a well-known bowhunting writer, and I arrived at our hilltop spotting position well after sunrise. Immediately we discovered a herd of deer, including five bucks, feeding on top of a flat hill in the bright sunlight. They stayed right there until mid-morning, their sleek backs shining in the sunlight, and then they slowly filtered down into a serviceberry patch on the north side of the hill and lay down.

On that same hunt, fellows running the hunt said we'd waste our time trying to spot animals early in the afternoon because the deer wouldn't start feeding until real late, just before dark. Being somewhat of a skeptic about such things, I went out to spot early one afternoon anyway. Even though it wouldn't get dark until 8 p.m. — this hunt took place in August — I started spotting deer at 3:30, 4 1/2 hours before dark. As soon as shadows started to get long, during that transition period between blistering day and cool evening, deer stirred in shaded draws and in the cool aspen groves and serviceberry patches. Granted they weren't out in the middle of open, sweltering sage flats, but nonetheless they were moving and visible.

In Nevada one day the temperature must have been 80 degrees, and the sun was intense. It was 2 p.m. and I was trying to take a nap because it was a cinch no deer would be feeding under those conditions. Suddenly a single little cloud drifted in front of the sun and the temperature must have dropped 20 degrees instantly. And just as suddenly deer seemed to pop out of every bush. On a steep hillside seemingly barren of deer only minutes before, I now counted 13 bucks. That lasted a half-hour, and then the cloud dissipated. Just as quickly the animals disappeared, and again I was looking at a seemingly barren hillside. It wasn't just my imagination, because my companion Mike Cupell said he'd witnessed the same thing in another canyon. Frequently on cool days or during cloudy periods, you'll catch deer out feeding any time during the day.

Under many circumstances, deer will feed well into the day. As I've said, heat and harassment are two reasons they bed early and seek cover for shade and concealment. In the absence of those two elements, they're liable to stay right out where you can see them at midday. Frequently, in reasonably cool weather, I've watched deer feed contentedly in the open until 10 a.m. and then lie down on the spot. During the day they'll get up to feed for a half-hour or an hour, and if you watch a good location long enough during the day, you'll spot these easy deer.

SPOTTING BEDDED BUCKS. Even when you can't locate feeding deer you might very well spot them bedded. It's not uncommon for bucks to bed right out in the middle of open flats. I suppose they do that because they feel secure surrounded by distance, much as antelope do. The only difference is that antelope lie in very short cover where they can see clearly in every direction. In contrast, deer often lie in high sage or other shrubs where they can't see out. They must feel securely hidden, but little do they know their antlers protrude above the bushes.

Never waste a cool day because bucks may be active and feeding all day long. Fog hardly presents ideal spotting conditions, but any cloud cover will keep air temperature down and deer will be moving. That's when you should be looking. (Photo by Pat Miller.)

With careful looking, you can locate bedded bucks simply by scanning sage flats or brush patches, looking for antlers. Concentrate on swales or pockets of higher brush where the sage, bitterbrush or other shrubs are lush and tall. Nothing will make you tingle faster than the sight of antler tips poking up from the brush, because you can just imagine what's lying right below them. Many times I've spotted deer during hot midday just by glassing for antlers.

In steep country, follow Dan Herrig's advice and start looking on north and east slopes where deer can find cool bedding shade all day. During hot weather I think deer definitely will gravitate to these cooler slopes to bed.

But don't give up if you don't find deer there. By no means do they bed only on north slopes. Almost as often I've spotted deer bedded on hot, dry south-facing slopes. When you're spotting in such country, look under any rock, bush or tree that provides even scant shade, and chances are you'll spot a deer there. One day Larry Jones and I walked to a cliff overlooking an open sage basin. There wasn't one tree in the entire basin, just big boulders and a mix of sage and other mountain shrubs. The time was 1 p.m., and the sun was intense on the south-facing side of the bowl. If we'd been strictly foot hunters, we'd have taken one look and hurried on. That place looked dead.

But we're eye hunters, so we found a shady spot and got out our lunches, and then we set up our spotting scopes to investigate. Not 2 minutes had passed before Larry had spotted a buck lying under a rock. In the next hour we'd spotted 18 bucks bedded on a south-facing slope in the middle of a blazing day. Many of the deer were lying in dug-out beds below boulders, and others lay in the shade of the tallest bushes.

Look for bedded bucks on ridges or benches where a breeze blowing uphill will cool them, and where they can command a good view of the surrounding country. In desert country where the only cover may be a few scattered juniper or mahogany trees, deer will develop traditional bedding sites, and the beds will be dug out several feet deep under some trees and rocks. When you find such places, remember them because you'll consistently see deer bedded there.

I've spotted lots of bedded bucks simply by glassing the shade under isolated trees. It doesn't take much of an eye to pick out these dark, shaded antlers against the sunlit background. The only problem here is that you can't see all the deer under this tree.

I've spotted lots of bedded deer by inspecting the shade under trees. Often a buck's shaded antlers will be silhouetted against sunlit ground beyond. Spotting bucks that way is most common in the desert where shade trees are scarce, but I've done it successfully in the high mountains, too.

Before sunrise one morning in Oregon's Wallowa Mountains, I watched several bucks feeding on an open sandy flat, but as the sun came up they drifted over a ridge out of sight. The ridge was open decomposed granite with only a few scattered, stunted pine trees toward the lower end. Possibly the deer would drift on downhill into heavy timber where they'd be tough to relocate, but bucks being what they are, I figured they'd stay up on the open ridge and bed in the shade of those sparse pines.

So I hiked right to the top of the ridge and started slinking downhill, glassing into the shade. I'd move 20 yards and sit down to glass carefully for 10 minutes, then move and glass, move and glass. I hadn't gone 200 yards when I saw antlers under a tree. A good-size 4-point lay in the shade under low-hanging pine limbs. I eventually got within 30 yards of that buck, and then shot over him.

A few days later Larry Jones came up to my camp. He'd been elk hunting and had taken a bull, so now he wanted to try for a deer. I pointed toward the ridge. "If I were you I'd go right to the top of that ridge and work down slowly and glass under every tree." Larry left camp at 8 a.m. At 2 p.m., he came strolling back into camp. A big grin told his story; he'd

Through years of constant use, beds had been dug out so deep under this mahogany tree I couldn't see the other two bucks until they stood up. The center buck has a spread of 35 inches or so. Unfortunately, I'd filled my tag with a much smaller buck the day before and could do nothing but snap a camera shutter on this one.

killed a buck, sure enough, as it lay in its bed, just below where I'd seen the 4-point a few days earlier.

THE MECHANICS OF SPOTTING

Speaking of Larry reminds me of another spotting story. One day we were driving up a road when Larry screeched to a halt.

"There's a deer," he said. "Standing by the big stump straight across the canyon. Now why do you think I saw that deer right there?" Again he was analyzing. And again I said the wrong thing.

"Because it looks like a deer."

Larry jerked off his hat and beat me severely with it. "You're sure a big help," he said.

Actually, it had taken a good eye to spot that deer at that distance, but I think Larry saw it only because he's had practice. As soon as his eye catches the least little part of a deer, he recognizes that as part of a deer.

EYE CATCHERS. Most articles on deer hunting suggest you look for horizontal lines, a black nose, twitching ears and so forth. I suppose that's good advice, and indeed you do have to know the characteristics of a deer to spot efficiently. I recall my frustration the first time I hunted whitetails after a long background of mule deer hunting. As we walked up a hill, my friend Dewey Haeder whispered, "There goes a good buck!" I saw nothing until the deer trotted into the open only 100 yards away. Then the movement caught my eye.

We hadn't climbed another 200 yards before Dewey pointed out two more bucks, and then he saw a fourth. Good grief. Was I blind?

It took me awhile to adapt my eyes to the appearance of those deer. Even in December, the whitetails looked much browner than the nearly charcoal mule deer, and they lacked the distinct white rump patch of mule deer. Also, the whitetails' antlers were much whiter. When I learned to look for ivory antlers and brown deer things improved considerably. In particular I discovered that a whitetail at rest holds its tail down, and in place of the white rump patch of a mule deer you can see a distinct white V along the outer edges of the tail. With my eye adjusted to these differences, I started spotting deer all over the place.

The same transition was required in Arizona. Larry Jones and I went down to hunt Coues deer, the diminutive Arizona whitetails. Again I felt blind until I learned that Coues deer are about half the size of mule deer and are dark grey. When I forgot about deer and concentrated on looking for mice bounding through the open oaks, I spotted lots of bucks.

I'm not sure anyone can tell you what to look for, although it may help you to study photos to learn the characteristics of each species. With mule deer you'll notice the distinct white rump, white down the insides of the legs, and a white muzzle contrasted sharply with a dark forehead and black nose, and, of course, big ears and antlers.

In late summer, mule deer will be reddish brown, and about September

1, as they're shedding velvet, their coats will turn charcoal grey. At any given time, some may be brown, some grey, and some half-and-half. By late September, they'll all be dark grey. On a sunny day, you often can see the body of a fat buck glistening like a Polish sausage, and you'll more likely recognize a distant buck by shine than by color.

EXPERIENCE. Learning these traits will help you to spot deer, but I think the ability to recognize them quickly comes from experience. I can tell you what they look like, but only by studying them in the field, over and over, will you develop a game eye. That's why Larry spotted that one deer instantly. It wasn't because of any particular technique. It was because he'd seen so many deer, that as soon as the image hit his eye his brain said, "Deer!" Like I said, he saw it because it looked like a deer.

SYSTEMATIC APPROACH. Some hunters suggest you divide the area you plan to spot into quadrants, or visualize graph paper laid over it so you can systematically glass back and forth to make sure you don't overlook any detail. That's probably good advice and I try to follow it, but in any given country some spots will be more attractive to deer than others, so I instinctively concentrate my looking on these prime places and skim over the marginal stuff.

There are two basic spotting methods. Either you can slowly and systematically pick apart an area, looking for any slight detail as you go, covering the area just once, but very thoroughly. Or you can scan more rapidly and look over the country many times.

The first method works best during midday when bucks are bedded, because they'll lie motionless and you have to inspect for minute detail to see them. But during feeding periods I prefer to move my binoculars (or scope) fairly rapidly, scanning the entire area, and then going over it again, and again, and again. My theory is that deer are easy to see if they're in the right position. When they're feeding they move around, changing position constantly, and a buck hidden behind a bush one minute will step into the open and become obvious the next. I can't see much sense in staring, trying to spot him behind that bush, when I can come back to that spot a few minutes later and see him easily.

TIME IS THE KEY. That doesn't mean you can get away with a quick once over. Whatever approach you take, time is the essence. You have to look for long periods. If you know roughly what a deer looks like, and you pick some good country, and if you spend long enough looking, you'll spot deer.

At each spotting location, you should spend a minimum of an hour sitting tight, studying the country, and in most cases you can't go wrong with 3 or 4 hours. That's especially true in broken, cliffy terrain with pockets of trees and shrubs. In that kind of country, deer can find a thousand places to hide, but if you systematically dissect a canyon side, you'll eventually spot most of the deer that are there.

Even in simpler country, though, you might need a lot of time to spot a buck. One time I saw a deer early in the morning, and when I looked away from the scope for a few minutes, the deer disappeared. That was at 8:30. I looked for a couple of hours, picking apart every bush and clump of grass. Could it be possible that buck was still there? Where could he hide?

One thing I've learned is that deer don't take off for no good reason. Unless you see a deer run away, you can assume he's close to where you last saw him. Assuring myself with that thought, I refused to give up and kept looking. Right at noon, after 3 1/2 hours, I finally respotted the buck as he stood up to stretch. I eventually stalked to within 25 yards of the big-antlered brute and got so shook up I shot 3 feet to the left.

I don't want to belabor the point, but putting in your time is so important it merits another story. Larry Jones and I had spotted a 25-inch 4-point, and Larry wanted to stalk him. But we made a mistake. We took our eyes off him, and he vanished. We climbed around to get different perspectives but we just couldn't see him. He'd slipped away.

But, no, we'd hunted enough to know deer don't run off without good reason. We were sure this one hadn't seen or smelled us.

"He's there," I said with assurance. "He's lying on that knob somewhere."

We peered another hour, changing position several times. How could he possibly hide that well in so little cover?

"Do you really think he's there?" I said.

"He's there," Larry said adamantly. Larry is a confident, patient hunter who doesn't know how to quit; he'll carry on after everyone else has returned to camp for a nap. "Let's look from one more spot."

We studied for 5 minutes, 10, then 15.

"There he is," Larry said. "See that rock with the red strip down the middle? Just above that you can see a tine."

"Sure enough," I agreed. "That's obvious enough. Once you see it."

And that's the point. Deer are obvious once you see them. It's just a matter of time.

CHAPTER 5

BEFORE THE STALK

Stalking. That word seems to intrigue hunters. When you view the stalking hunter, you're reminded of a powerful, stealthy mountain lion creeping along a cliff, moving yet unmoving. It seems the stalking animal exemplifies everything a serious big game hunter would like to become. Stalking has a reputation of being the highest form of hunting art.

Yet at the same time, I consider it the simplest. Certainly stalking presents a challenge absent from more sedate forms of hunting like stand hunting. Like any productive form of hunting, stalking indeed demands patience and fortitude. In contrast to many methods, however, you know the exact location of the buck you want before you waste an ounce of energy going after him, and you can plan a strategy that's almost guaranteed. That's what makes stalking easy.

And that's what makes it sure. You often read about the rifle hunter who spots a buck at 400 yards and just can't get any closer so he's forced to take a long shot. In reality what he's saying is that he wouldn't take the time or exert the energy to get any closer. As you well know, spotting a buck at 400 yards might mark the end of a hunt for a rifleman, but it only marks the beginning for an archer. You must get within 50 yards or less to hope for a shot. And I've virtually never seen a situation in which I couldn't do just that.

YOU CAN DO IT

CLIFF BUCKS. Sometimes the potential in stalking surprises even me. One time in Oregon's Blue Mountains I saw three fine bucks, all 4-points in the 25-inch class, feeding up through a rock slide. They topped out onto a cliff and started feeding on a little bench. It looked impossible to stalk them there. To get to them I'd have to cover 200 yards of open meadow and then climb 50 yards straight up through a cliff covered with loose rock. "Get serious, man," I thought. "That's crazy."

On the other hand, if I did get up there, just think. A 30-yard shot at a great buck. That was strong incentive. Try!

It worked. From the time I reached the base of the cliff, it took me a half-hour to climb to the top, moving an inch at a time. When I peaked over, a cluster of antlers bobbing contentedly met me right at eye level. These big boys had no idea they'd been snuck. My rear end tingled and my palms sweated ice. "Don't blow it now, kid!" I thought. My arrow struck with a solid thunk, and I was elated. But after the deer had run off apparently unscathed, I went over to find my arrow planted in a rotten log between me and the deer. Well, nobody's perfect. At least I'd got a 30-yard shot.

PRAIRIE BUCKS. Another time, while taking pictures, I spotted four huge bucks lying out on a rolling hillside covered with nothing but shin-high grass. "No way," I thought. "Forget it." But something down inside said, "You can't do it if you don't try." So I tried and ended up crawling within 40 yards of those bucks and shooting a roll of film before they got wise and split. I'd have had a good bow shot on them.

If you go into it with the attitude that "It cain't be done," then it probably cain't. But if you figure you can do it, you can. Stalking Rule No. 1: You'll never succeed if you don't try.

BASIC DECISIONS

BEDDED BUCKS. Before you do any stalking, you have to decide how to go about it. When Glenn Helgeland, who's hunted primarily for midwestern whitetails, and I spotted a herd of bucks on a hilltop one morning, we were eager. Who wouldn't want to get right after bucks like that? We watched them for an hour or more until they'd bedded in a cluster of serviceberry bushes.

"Let's go on back to the cabin and have breakfast, and we'll come back after them this afternoon," I suggested.

Glenn didn't come right out and call me crazy, but I'm sure he questioned my sanity. At any rate we went on back, ate breakfast, rested, shot our bows and finally returned at 1 p.m. We came in from below and slipped over the backside of the hill. At 20 yards I spotted antlers in the shade next to a serviceberry bush. As I looked around for a place to hide and wait, the buck got up and started feeding right toward me. I drew and waited and he finally turned broadside at 30 feet and I thumped him.

That's the classic approach to spotting and stalking. In ideal cases you spot a buck early in the morning and watch until he lies down. Once a buck beds, he'll stay right there all day. Occasionally he'll get up to stretch

I think the best approach, particularly in open, flat country like this, is to wait for a buck to bed for the day. That approach gives you plenty of time to stalk. I watched this buck lie down out in open grass, and then I crawled within 40 yards. He doesn't know he's been had.

and nibble some twigs, but he won't move far. That fact provides the element you must have for successful stalking — time. After you've watched a buck bed in the morning, you have virtually all day until late afternoon to get within bow range. I've spent as much as 4 to 5 hours stalking different bucks. My friend Cliff Dewell said he took 8 hours getting within 30 yards of one deer he wanted badly.

You have other advantages over bedded deer. In many cases, a deer's view is restricted by the very cover he thinks is hiding him, and as he's lying down, a buck necessarily must face one direction, so in essence he has a blind side, which gives you a good approach route. In steep country, deer most often face downhill, so as long as the wind is right, you can stalk down from above without being seen. These facts give you the edge you need to stalk that buck.

FEEDING DEER. In contrast, stalking a feeding buck can be tough to impossible. The deer is moving so you have to move fast to keep up, and because he's standing, he can see well in all directions. He's not blindsided. In open, flat sage country I've tried stalking and ambushing feeding bucks dozens of times, and I've given it up as a bad job. Now I wait for them to bed in the morning, and I rarely try to stalk them late in the afternoon when they're getting up to feed for the evening.

Broken country presents a different story. In high mountains, cliffy desert ranges, breaks or badlands, terrain itself often provides good cover and you can sneak on a feeding buck confidently. Before sunrise in

Oregon's Eagle Cap Wilderness, for example, I saw two bucks feeding at the top of a meadow. I knew those bucks would be hard to find once they bedded in heavy timber surrounding the meadow, and it was early enough in the morning so they'd keep feeding long enough to give me some time. I decided to go after them immediately rather than waiting for them to bed.

A shallow draw cut up through the middle of the meadow. I picked out a big flat rock in the draw below the bucks and set that as my goal — if I could get there, I'd shoot. Coming up through timber at the bottom of the meadow, I slipped into the draw and tiptoed from one rock to another, crouched over, always keeping one hand on the ground for balance. With each step my knees shook more violently and my palms started sweating. That happens when I'm confident of getting a shot. I got to that flat rock and shot the bigger of the two bucks right at 7 a.m., 15 minutes after I'd first spotted them. You can stalk feeding bucks if conditions are right.

Harold Boyack, who has placed a number of bucks high in the Pope and Young Record book, said he prefers to stalk feeding bucks. He watches them from a distance and tries to predict their route. Then he circles around and intercepts them as they move from feeding to bedding grounds or vice versa, and he figures his chances for a good shot are a lot better if that buck is moving toward him than if he's moving toward the buck. In some cases where terrain permits, this approach can be a lot more deadly than stalking bedded deer. You have to read each situation individually.

In broken country like this, the terrain itself offers good cover and in many cases you can stalk bucks as they feed below cliffs or in little draws or bowls. You have to judge each situation on its own merits to decided whether to wait for a buck to bed or to stalk him as he feeds.

PLANNING A STALK

Now let's figure you've set yourself in a good glassing position early in the morning and lo and behold, yonder feeds a buck you'd sure like to kill. He's nibbling on bitterbrush out on a desert flat, and through your spotting scope you can see him chewing and scratching his back with his chin. It's like you were sitting right there beside him, watching his every move. As the sun tops the horizon and hits his back, he shines like a hog. Man, you've dreamed about this sight since last winter. You can't wait to put yourself in that picture, to see yourself crawling toward antler tips in the sage, to watch that arrow striking home. The very idea gives you the shivers.

But take it easy. "Hurry" is the most dangerous word in bowhunting. In reviewing my hunting records for the past 15 years — I've got a stack of diaries 2 feet high — I discover my most common mistake, and the one that kept me from bagging deer most often, was impatience. I got in a hurry. That applies to all stages of spotting and stalking, and it starts the moment you've spotted a buck. Take your time. Be patient. This is the time to plan.

For the sake of discussion, let's assume you've decided to wait for this buck to bed. The same procedure applies for all stalking, but it will take more or less time, depending on circumstances. But one truth applies to any stalk — if you get in a hurry you'll blow it. Think first.

PLAN YOUR ROUTE. In some cases route planning may be simple. On those Eagle Cap bucks feeding in the meadow, a deep draw led right to them. Seeing that didn't take much time.

But rarely is it that simple. I've wasted days worth of time and blown many stalks looking for deer that were right where they were supposed to be. In one case Laura and I spotted a buck about a mile away, lying in sagebrush, and I went after him immediately. Half-cocked. Arriving on the scene, I looked around for 2 hours and couldn't find the stinker, so I walked clear back to the original spotting position and, sure enough, the buck was still right there. I walked clear back out there and snuck within 30 yards of him. I could well have done without that extra 2-mile walk, though.

NEW PERSPECTIVE. The real problem comes when you've changed position. As you sit in one spot, looking at the country and watching your prize buck, everything looks clear and straight forward. As soon as you move and get a different perspective, the rocks, trees and other features all look different, and pretty soon you're asking, "Now, was he by that tree? Or was it that one?"

In Oregon's Blue Mountains I saw a huge, reddish-brown buck feeding in a place I later named Buck Hollow because this place so regularly attracted bucks. My first look at Big Brownie got me all excited. He was big. And stalking him in that hollow looked like a cinch, so I went right after him without further ado.

Take time to plan. Unless you or someone else spooks a deer he's not going anywhere and will give you plenty of time. Use your spotting scope to study the buck's position and the terrain around him to plan a foolproof stalking route.

The terrain was ideal and getting within spitting range was no big problem, but when I got there, he was gone. "Drat it. I couldn't possibly have spooked him," I thought. But as I analyzed the country there, I realized my mistake. From my spotting position up high, it looked like Buck Hollow was right at the bottom of the canyon. But close up, I discovered it was actually well up the side of the hill. Brownie probably had seen me coming down, because he wasn't where I thought he was. With some time spent planning to start with, I'd have figured out the lay of the country and might have been packing meat that afternoon.

The longer the distance from you to the buck, the more critical this becomes. Over a distance of a mile, you'll have trouble gauging all the dips and draws and swales between you and a deer, and it takes some study.

But even at short range you have to plan. One day in Nevada's Ruby Mountains I walked over a ridge and instantly noticed a big gray buck lying in a willow patch no more than 150 yards below me. He was facing straight away, a tailor-made setup. I backed slowly out of his sight over the ridge and came down directly above him.

He should have been within 50 to 60 yards, but he'd vanished. I looked around for 10 minutes but couldn't see him. "He must have spooked," I thought. But just to double check I went back to my original position to look again, and there he was, lying right in the same spot. But now he was looking my way, and as soon as I stepped into view, he jumped up and trotted off. He'd been in an ideal stalking position, if only I'd taken a few extra minutes from the beginning to mark him better.

DRAW A MAP. As you plan, study the land in detail to locate big rocks, gnarled trees, ravines, dead bushes — anything you can identify positively when you get close to the deer.

And then draw a map. That might seem silly now, but memory is notoriously unreliable, and when you've changed position, you'll be questioning yourself, wondering if you've really got your landmarks straight. After goofing up a few times, I started carrying a small pad and pencil, and now I sit right there and look through my binoculars and scope, and sketch out a map of the country around the buck. These maps have contributed to more than one successful stalk.

USE YOUR COMPASS. You also can mark a buck with a compass reading. One time I watched a deer disappear over a long rim. From my position I couldn't pick out any good landmark along that rim to mark the buck, so I took a compass bearing on the spot where the deer disappeared. Then I walked to the rim and took a reverse bearing on the spot from which I'd been glassing. When the needle lined up perfectly I started looking over the rim for the buck and found him within 100 yards. The compass has helped guide me to numerous bucks, especially featureless country with few good landmarks.

SPOT THE SPOILERS. Another good reason for careful looking before you stalk is other deer. Quite frankly, if you could always find single bucks, you'd have no trouble killing deer. It's other deer — spoilers — that mess things up.

Above timberline one day I saw two fine bucks feeding on willows in a shallow ravine. Getting a shot at them was guaranteed. Confidently, and without further looking, I slipped down through the timber, but just at the edge of the ravine, I walked into another big buck. He exploded from the brush almost at my feet and left me fluttering like an aspen leaf in a gale. And, of course, he took the other bucks with him as he bounded away. Always take time to spot these spoilers before you begin a stalk so you can work around them. You'll save yourself a lot of frustration.

Incidentally, or actually not so incidentally, you'd better look for cows and other livestock. Most good western deer country is heavily grazed, and during summer bow seasons deer share their range with livestock. Range cattle are nearly as wild as deer, so take time to spot the cows, and go to great lengths to avoid them or you'll end up with a stampede you won't believe.

WIND. It should go without saying, but wind has to be the most critical factor in any big game hunting, so as you plan a stalk, judge the wind. Obviously you must approach a buck from the downwind side, or at least cross wind.

In high mountains and most broken canyon country, wind can be totally unpredictable, and I think deer have this figured out and know where to hang out for safety. In a high range near Beaver, Utah, two bucks lay at the head of a draw. I started to approach them from one side but the wind was sucking around my side of the hill right into their draw. So I backed off and circled clear around to approach from the opposite direction. And again the wind came right down my back into the draw. Don't ask me how that could be, but the wind blew directly into that draw from all directions. The only possible way to approach those deer was from below, and they lay facing that way. Those bucks were safe.

Not all deer country is that bad, of course, and with patience you not only can figure out wind patterns, but you can put the wind to work for you. In open, flat country you may be able to judge wind at the buck's location by what it's doing at yours. In broken country, or when a storm is producing blustery swirls, you probably can't. With your binoculars or scope, watch grass or moss hanging from trees near the buck to get an idea of the wind's disposition there.

Wind presents a good reason for midday stalking. Early in the morning a breeze will drift down canyon. If you can get to a buck as the wind drifts down, you're okay, but as the sun comes up the breeze will begin to shift, and if you get caught during this transition period, you've had it. By mid-morning it will stabilize again, and often, especially in the desert, you'll get a fairly steady, reliable wind from 10 a.m. until late afternoon. That's the best time to stalk. In desert rimrock country, you'll almost always get a strong uphill wind during the day, and nothing could be more ideal.

That's strong argument in favor of biding your time. If you wait until the wind shifts and settles into its reliable midday pattern, you've won half the stalking battle.

As you plan a stalking route, try to locate all deer in the vicinity of the buck you want so you can avoid them. Blundering into unseen deer will end your stalk in a hurry.

Before you stalk, assess the wind. On clear days it often will get steady during the day, but with a coming storm, as shown here, the wind could be shifting. You might as well stay away from a deer under bad wind conditions.

CALM DEER. Not only does the wind normally settle down during the day, but the deer do, too, and that's another strong reason for waiting.

When deer first lie down, they're still a little fidgety and may get up and move around, but once they've bedded for awhile, they seem to relax and become a little more stalkable.

Cliff Dewell specializes in stalking desert bucks, and he has strong opinions about waiting.

"I never go right after a buck as soon as he lies down," Dewell said. "I wait for at least 45 minutes or an hour to let him settle in. I used to feel like I was on a time schedule and had to get right after them or they'd get up and move on. I'd nearly run for fear they'd leave. But now I know that's fiddlesticks. They're not going anywhere, and the longer you give them, the more they'll relax.

"I'd rather stalk a buck at 3 or 4 o'clock in the afternoon than at 10 a.m. or noon," Dewell said. "He's been lying there all day undisturbed and has relaxed as much as he ever will. I think that's when my chances are best."

THE STAGE IS SET

At this point the stage is set. You've got a buck in sight, and you've taken time to plan. Nothing is guaranteed in hunting, and I make you no promises now. But I'll say with confidence, based on my own experience, that if you've done it all right up to this point, you've laid the foundation for one of the surest bucks you'll ever hunt.

CHAPTER 6

CLOSING IN

The whole purpose of a stalk is to approach a buck undetected. Some guys like to spot a buck and then go back to camp and get the whole crew and surround the buck and start launching arrows when the fleeing animal tries to break through the line. Occasionally they get lucky and hit one, but the chances of making a clean kill are slim, and they're just as slim for any one hunter to selectively kill the trophy buck of his choice.

Other hunters just seem to muddle through the woods, aimlessly looking for deer, hoping for a shot, operating by no plan at all. Apparently they figure if they cover enough ground and see enough animals, they'll sooner or later get lucky. That used to be my philosophy, and commonly now I run into hunters who operate the same, aimless way. Some guys at the Canyon Creek archery unit in Oregon seemed to have that problem. They'd seen a number of bucks, but they were discouraged.

"The deer here are so wild we can't get close," one of them said. "We're lucky to get within 80 yards."

"What does he expect?" I thought later. "Tame deer?"

Most deer ARE wild, but that doesn't mean you can't get close. Certainly if they know you're there, you've had it; but if they don't, it doesn't matter how spooky they are. They won't run from anything. The fact is, if you're sneaky enough, you can get within bow range of the wildest bucks.

The essence of stalking, I think, is to pick out the buck you want and to take him one-on-one. Look at it this way. As you study a buck through your scope, you can watch him carry on normal life. He'll nibble the tips of bitterbrush, chew his cud, scratch his back, stretch, doze. It's as if you're sitting right there beside him as he carries on without a care in the world. That sight is the thing that really turns me on; that IS hunting. I almost get depressed anymore to see a buck suspicious, sniffing the air, staring, listening, walking stiff legged, ears back. When bucks act like that, something is wrong. I've blown it. The whole idea behind stalking is to put yourself in the picture of serenity you see through your spotting scope without changing it. If you do everything right, the picture will remain unchanged until the very thunk! of your arrow.

Certainly, two people who can work together can direct each other with hand signals or, in cases, push deer to each other, but stalking allows little room for the gang hunt. When it's just you and a buck out on the lonely heights of a distant mountain, and you're pitting your skills against his senses, one-on-one, you've discovered the essence of hunting.

RELOCATING A BUCK

Now let's figure you've got a buck bedded down, or maybe feeding below a cliff where you can sneak up on him, you've planned your route, taking the wind and other animals into account, and you're ready to stalk. If you've picked your spotting position well, you can slip out of sight quickly and begin to circle downwind of your chosen buck. At this stage you often can move fairly fast, because you probably have a ridge or hill between you and the buck and are totally out of sight. Even at that, be cautious. You could still run into other animals and start a stampede.

When you reach a point where you think you can see the buck again, you face possibly the toughest part of stalking — respotting the animal. That might seem questionable since you already know he's there, but don't kid yourself. If he's feeding he has probably moved, and you've got to be sharp to see him before he sees you.

If he was bedded, he might have got up to feed or stretch, and he could be looking around and catch you off guard. Even if he's still bedded right where you last saw him, you could have trouble. You're probably approaching 180 degrees from your original spotting position, and from this viewpoint nothing will look the same. Besides, deer commonly lie with their backs tight against bushes or rocks — which is probably the way you're coming in — and even if you know exactly where a buck is lying, you may not be able to see him.

GLASS. Binoculars aren't just for long-range stuff. Use them now. Before moving closer, glass each twig, branch and rock. When you're satisfied you've seen everything there is to see, take a step and glass again. You've got to see that deer before he sees you, so look hard. In many cases you'll notice only the tine of an antler, the top of his back, a leg, a nose, a hoof, a twitching tail. Take a half step and glass 5 minutes, then step and glass. In particular examine each new view of the skyline, because you'll often see antlers silhouetted against the sky. If you take

Here's a deer's eye view of me during the process of relocating a buck. Even at close range, you must use your binoculars continuously. Take a step and glass, step and glass. You may spot only an antler tip or a flicking ear, but if you take enough time you'll respot a buck before he sees you.

enough time, you'll spot the smallest detail that will give the buck away.

While hunting whitetails in Idaho, I slipped into the downwind side of a pine grove where several bucks hung out and started glassing ahead. Right next to the ground, 20 to 30 yards away, I saw a white line. It didn't look like any part of a deer, yet it caught my eye. It moved. I studied it. Pretty soon a 10-point buck took a step and revealed part of an antler. He was grazing, and the white line was the white band across his nose. That's the kind of detail you'll spot if you take time to look.

DON'T GIVE UP. If you don't spot the buck right off, don't panic. Be cool. He's there. You just can't see him. Keep looking. This point is so important it has become one of my cardinal rules of stalking: Unless you've seen a deer run off, HE'S THERE. More than once I've ignored that rule and regretted it.

The classic example took place in Oregon's Blue Mountains on a blustery, day in September. Occasional rays of sun stabbed through the black clouds with gentle warmth, but mostly the clouds won out, and I felt comfortable in a wool shirt and wool sock hat. Perched on the south side of a jagged canyon looking north, I spotted a decent 4-point.

"Ah, man, look at that," I said to myself. "Nice buck. That's the one for me."

About that time a massive set of antlers rose from the plum bushes behind the first buck. They reminded me of moose antlers, so grossly did they dwarf the other buck's rack. I quickly set up the spotting scope and stared. Never had I seen such an animal. I'd crawl to the moon for a buck like that. For 15 minutes I studied the animal. He was, and still is, the biggest buck I've even seen. The stalk was on!

The deer were feeding in plum bushes a half-mile straight across the canyon, but I'd have to hike to the bottom and up the other side to reach them, a good mile hike.

That took an hour. During that time several snow squalls blew through and the wind whipped this way and that, and it seemed sure the bucks would smell me. To add further doubt, when I got on the bucks' side, the layout wasn't so clear. There were several plum patches, and I couldn't be sure where the deer had been. As I hunkered under a tree waiting for a seething snow storm to blow by, I felt sure I'd come to the right patch, but there was no way of knowing for sure, and I couldn't see any sign of the deer.

About that time a grouse jumped up on a rock 15 feet away, clucking, tempting me. I was freezing and hungry, and roast grouse seemed like just what the doctor would order under such conditions. My mind started playing tricks. With the wind swirling as it was, the deer surely had smelled me, and besides I couldn't be positive this was the right plum patch. I'd looked around thoroughly and couldn't find them. Surely they were gone. Soon I'd convinced myself the bucks had taken off and jerked out my blunt practice arrow to chunk the grouse. As the arrow clanged off a rock, a sickening explosion took place in the nearest plum bushes. Huge antlers erupted 20 yards away as the two bucks sprang to their feet and vacated.

Unless you've seen them run off, KNOW they're still there and keep looking.

THE PHILOSOPHY OF GETTING CLOSE

Relocating a buck in one sense is a mechanical process that involves moving, looking, moving, looking, but more than that it's a philosophy. Like a good road hunter, you've got to operate in compound low. As the saying goes, "Impatience goes before the fall," and that's definitely true in stalking. Nine out of 10 times, when I've blown stalks it's because I've gotten impatient and moved too fast.

TIME. If you could sum up the essence of successful stalking — or realistically, all bowhunting for deer — in one word, it would be "time." Take time. Don't hurry. I mentioned this same point in regard to spotting deer and again in planning a stalk, but it's worth emphasis again here. In all bowhunting, time is the essence. Don't force your hand. Virtually never will you gain an advantage by moving fast. Oh, it may happen. You could see a buck walking toward a saddle, and by running you could get into position to ambush him there. But most times fast movement will hinder far more than it will help. Either you'll make noise and the buck will hear you, or he'll catch you moving, or you'll go too far and get upwind of him. Something will go wrong. You just don't have enough control when you hurry.

One time I asked my friend Don Pritchett why he'd been so successful as a bowhunter. He said it was because he'd learned to "flow."

"Nothing moves fast in Nature," Pritchett said. "In an undisturbed outdoor world everything moves slowly, quietly, calmly. The only thing that moves faster than the game animals is a predator. Deer will spot anything moving fast. There's a certain flow in the woods, and to be consistent in bowhunting you can't break that flow."

THE MOVING STAND. Consider a different perspective. A survey by the American Archery Council showed that between 1974 and 1983, overall bowhunting success in the U.S. rose from 5.2 percent to 11 percent. In writing an article on that subject, I asked many veterans of the archery industry why success had gone up. "Tree stands" was one of the most common responses, and hunter surveys support that opinion. In some eastern states, nearly 80 percent of the bow-killed whitetails are taken by hunters using tree stands. Average shooting distance is just under 20 yards.

That brings up the question: Why do tree stands make hunters so deadly? I think it's because a stand allows a person to implant himself in a deer's home ground undetected. A stand hunter gets in place under cover of darkness; he perches above a deer's eye level where he'll rarely be seen; he's off the ground where deer most likely won't smell him; he remains motionless and lets the deer do the moving, so he virtually always sees them first. He's like a sparrow perched on a branch, watching the world go by, and he's got deer at his mercy.

This isn't a sales pitch for stand hunting, but the fact is foot hunters can learn a lesson from it. If you can implant yourself in a deer's environs — just as a stand hunter does — without being seen, smelled or heard, you can get good shots just as well as the guy up a tree. To do that you must duplicate the aspects of stand hunting that make it deadly. In essence, you take a moving stand. You move, but you do it so slowly deer can't see you move; you remain motionless long enough to see all movement, to discern all detail.

NO ADVANTAGE. My journals record well over a hundred stalks, and they make one thing clear — I've virtually never gained an advantage by hurrying, but I've sure blown a few chances by doing it.

Here's one of many examples. In a big alpine bowl carpeted with all sorts of lush bushes I spotted a group of 10 bucks, and among them was a 4-point with a spread close to 30 inches, the kind of buck I'd work long and hard to kill. He limped slightly, so I named him Old Gimpy.

As on most stalks I got within 100 yards easily, but then a herd of cattle blocked my way. I tried crawling past them, but one curious, turkey-necked steer spotted me and, of course, started a stampede. Fortunately, the cows ran downhill away from the deer, but still the bucks got suspicious. Looking through a screen of aspen trees, I could see some of them walking stiff-legged up the hill.

My mind started whirling: "There goes my chance. May never see that buck again. If I can get into that draw I can slip ahead of them and get a shot as they file past. Hurry. Hurry!"

I'd taken a few quick steps through the aspens when movement caught my eye. It was Old Gimpy. He'd been feeding right next to the aspen trees, and he hadn't even moved when those cows took off. Here he stood, at 25 yards, staring at a dumb bowhunter who'd come sprinting by. I tried to raise my bow to draw, but he was gone. If I'd just sat down and taken my time to let things calm down, and then proceeded slowly, I'd have seen him first and got the shot.

SLOW PAYS. At the extreme, rarely have I lost an opportunity by moving slow, and in most cases it has worked wonders. I could cite dozens of examples, but one stands out in particular. It took place in Utah. Two bucks lay in the sagebrush on a ridgetop. I had to cross an open hill from below and was about halfway across when some does spotted me from a nearby aspen patch. They stomped around so I just sat down and waited. They finally left, and I sneaked on. Every couple of feet I'd stop to glass the brush ahead and finally spotted the antlers of two bucks, and crawled within 70 yards.

Given the wind direction and cover, getting closer seemed impossible, so I settled in to wait. Something would break sooner or later. About an hour later the bucks got up and wandered down the hill and up the far side where they fed for awhile and then bedded down again, facing me. To get off this hillside I had to walk a quarter-mile across an open sagebrush slope, in plain view of the bucks. That seemed impossible, too, but by moving very slowly I made progress without catching their eye, and an hour later got out of their sight in the bottom of a draw.

The wind was blowing uphill, so I decided to go above them and come down from behind, but I got into slide rock and had to move rocks to assure solid footing. It took me 2 hours to cross above them, because one of them heard me and kept looking up the hill my way. To make a long story short, I finally came down behind the bucks, 5 1/2 hours after this whole thing had started. At that point, the bucks got up and walked right to me. I centered the 25-yard sight pin on the 4-point's chest and released. Would you believe, I shot over him?

To say the least, that was a disappointing ending after so much time and discipline, but I had to feel satisfied with the stalk. It worked only because I'd been patient and refused to hurry.

MORE THOUGHTS ON RELOCATING

SOUNDING OFF. If you've planned well you may be able to tell just from landmarks exactly where a buck is, and if you've followed my suggestion about the compass, you can take a compass line on the spot you were glassing from and get yourself within bow range of a deer, even if

Cliff Dewell has successfully stalked many desert bucks. If he has trouble relocating a buck, he hides in the brush and softly bleats on a predator call. He also uses the call to get a buck up for the shot.

you can't see him.

Cliff Dewell offers another suggestion. He likes to get within 30 yards or less to shoot, and to do that he must know exactly where a buck is lying. If he gets within 60 or 80 yards and still can't pinpoint the animal, he'll hide and bleat softly on a predator call, just enough make the buck curious. Invariably a deer will get up to investigate a sound like this, but when it can't see anything amiss it will relax and lie back down. Then you know the buck's exact position and can finish your stalk confidently. Just make sure you're well hidden when you blow that call. And don't move!

Two hunters working together can help each other. My friend Larry Jones guided me in on this buck, and when he saw the deer go down, Larry was much more excited than I was.

SIGNALS. I've said that hunting alone is the way to go, and that opinion still stands, but I have to admit that compatible partners can help each other if they'll sacrifice their own hunting time to work for each other. Laura helped guide me in on my first buck killed at Hart Mountain many years ago. She could see the animal from her side of the canyon, but he was screened from me by a low-hanging juniper. She motioned me to move first one way, and then the other until I was on course toward the buck. Then she signalled that all was well, and I proceeded with confidence.

My friend Larry Jones and I have worked out fairly detailed hand signals. When we've located a buck we want, one of us stays at the spotting position as the other stalks. The spotter has the deer and the stalker in sight all the time, and he can guide the stalker right to the deer. If he points one way or the other, that tells the stalker the buck is that direction. If he waves his hand in a circle over his head, that means the buck has got up to feed. If he bends over and touches his toes, the buck has moved downhill. Arms held in a big circle means everything is okay, keep going. If the spotter pretends he's shooting a bow, that means the stalker had better nock an arrow and get ready because something is about to happen. If the spotter waves his arms violently, it means the buck has spooked and the stalk is off.

With this method we virtually can talk to each other at long range, and we've found that watching your partner can be more exciting than doing it yourself. One time Larry and I spotted several bucks on a rocky hillside. One particularly fine buck lay down under a huge boulder. It was my turn to stalk so, while Larry stayed at the spotting position to guide me in, I circled above the buck to get the wind in my favor, and then slipped in quietly. Frequently I looked at Larry through my binoculars to see how things looked. He motioned me across, then down, and then he gave me the circled arms. Okay.

Just above the buck's rock, I slipped off my boots to complete the stalk in my socks. As quietly as a cat on wet grass, I walked within 15 yards of the buck's rock, nocked an arrow, and stood ready to shoot. For some reason, the deer chose just that moment to feed and he walked into the open just below me, facing straight away. I drew slowly, aimed and released a perfect arrow. It all seemed so simple. The deer sprinted 200 yards and tumbled down the hill.

Larry had watched it all and came on the run, hollering and smiling. He slapped me on the back and pumped my hand.

"That was fantastic!" he went on. "A perfect stalk. I could see nothing but legs and antlers as he rolled down the hill!"

I felt kind of silly. He was far more excited than I was.

TURNABOUT. A couple of years later the role was reversed, when we spotted a buck bedded under a cliff. This time it was his turn to stalk, so I stayed up above to guide as he moved in. We'd carefully marked the buck and Larry homed right on him, so mostly I signalled that everything was okay.

Watching Larry through the spotting scope reminded me of watching a crime show on TV. I could see Larry enter the picture, and just below him was the unsuspecting buck looking out over the valley. The organ music began to crescendo as Larry stepped to the edge of the cliff and peeked over. But Larry backed off and tiptoed down the hill a few yards. He'd come out just a hair too high. The tension was building. When would the homeowner discover the burglar?

Before he stepped to the edge of the cliff a second time, Larry pulled an arrow from his quiver, drew his bow a couple of times to loosen up and peeked over. This time I could see his knees tense. He could see the buck. He would shoot.

He leaned out as far as possible and drew his bow. The limbs lurched and instantly the buck jumped up and started running uphill. Even at that distance, more than a quarter-mile, I could see blood. The deer ran 100 yards, crashed to the ground and rolled down.

I ran down the hill, yelling and screaming, and began beating Larry on the back and pumping his hand. Watching him stalk the buck was one of my greatest thrills in deer hunting, but Larry seemed to be taking it all in stride. I felt kind of silly. I was far more excited than he was.

CHAPTER 7

THE STALK

With time and caution, you'll eventually relocate that buck. You might see the whole deer as he feeds out in open sage or on a cliffy bench. If he's in the clear, he's unaware, and he's within range, your task is simple. You shoot.

Rarely will that be the case, however. Commonly you'll re-spot a buck from 100 yards away or more, and in a position that allows no shot. You may see only antler tines in the brush, or part of his rump under a tree. Or you might not see the buck at all, only the rock or bush where you know he's bedded. Whatever the case, you come to a point when you know exactly where the buck is. Now you've got to close that gap and maneuver for a clear shot. You should get within 50 yards maximum, and better yet, 20 to 30. That's your assignment.

Mission impossible? No way. Once you've spotted a buck in stalkable position, moved around to get the wind on him, and then relocated him so you know his exact position, you've mastered the hard parts. Oh, I won't say all stalking is simple. It takes some energy and control, but with time it can be done. After you've read my approach, you might think, "That's too hard. It takes too much patience." Yet you'd sit in a tree stand for hours waiting for a buck you THINK might come along. Sure stalking takes patience, but you KNOW what lies at the end of the trail. This is a sure thing, so go for it.

GETTING PAST THE RADAR

In the previous chapters, I dwelt at length on taking your time, not hurrying, flowing with Nature, and so forth, so I won't belabor it here. Just consider anything said there as doubly important here. Slow movement and time form the core of a good stalk.

To understand why, consider a buck as a radar screen. Three of his senses — smell, hearing and sight — form a sensory barrier, and your task is to get inside that barrier without touching off the alarm. No jet can blast through an enemy's radar network without being detected, and you can't blast through a buck's sensory radar without getting caught. You have to sneak through, and to do that you have to understand the nature of the radar.

SMELL

Without question, smell is a deer's most infallible sense. Loren Butler, who makes his living studying scents and animals' reactions to them, said the sense of smell is an animal's only INDEPENDENT means of alarm. In other words, if a buck sees movement, he probably won't run; he'll listen and watch until he confirms what he's seen. If he hears something out of the ordinary, he won't bolt either; he'll watch and listen for further details. Sure, if a deer sees you walking on the skyline he doesn't need a double-take to know you're bad news. But if he just senses a strange sight or noise he can't identify, he'll often hold tight for confirmation.

With smell, tain't so. One whiff of human stench, and bango, he's gone. So you don't have any leeway. You simply can't let a buck smell you.

COVERUP SCENTS. Hunters ofter ask what I think about coverup scents. Frankly I don't think much about them. Loren Butler explained that scent is a physical substance just like smoke, only it's invisible. Like other physical substances, it's cumulative and can build up on your clothes and body. In other words, the longer you go without a bath, the worse you smell.

You probably already knew that, but here's the important point — coverup scents don't reduce your smell. They simply flood an area with their own aroma to overpower the human odor. Because skunk scent is so noxious, we humans figure it'll drown out any kind of smell, but as Butler points out, humans are nearly odor blind. He said a human's nose has about 10 million receptors, compared to hundreds of millions in the noses of animals. Not only can animals detect minute odors at long distances, but they can sort out a complex mixture of smells. The stronger your odor, the harder it is to mask.

Under some conditions, masking scents probably work. In stand hunting you can avoid working up a sweat, and if you've taken a bath and washed your clothes, you can eliminate most human odor. Then you can flood the area around your stand with a natural scent, and deer might not smell you.

But that's not true in hunting on foot. If you're camped out, you won't

You have to monitor the wind continuously to make a stalk work. The flame on a butane lighter helps you detect the slightest breeze.

be able to shower and wash your clothes regularly. And you'll climb long miles to reach your hunting country, and you'll swelter under a blazing sun. You'll get raunchy, and you can't help it. In my opinion, you can't mask that kind of B.O., and Loren Butler agrees.

"There's no way you can mask a 24-hour accumulation of body odor," he said. And that's from a guy who sells masking scents.

KEEPING THE ODOR DOWN. You might be able help your own cause to some degree. Cliff Dewell and Harold Boyack, both fine deer hunters, keep scent to a minimum. They take off their hunting clothes outside of camp to prevent infecting them with camp smell — bacon grease, soap, smoke — and they seal them in a bag with native plants, such as sage or pine, to impregnate the cloth with natural odors. And they bathe as often as possible during a hunt to prevent an accumulation of B.O. With these steps they can hold their odor to a minimum, and they think this helps.

Loren Butler recommends washing each day with a nonperfumed, nonallergenic soap and wearing clean clothes. If you have to hike hard to your hunting area, he suggests taking a clean T-shirt and a solution of baking soda and water in a wineskin. When you reach your destination and have cooled off, rinse your body with the soda solution and put on the clean shirt. This helps reduce odor considerably.

STAY DOWNWIND. These ideas are valuable, particularly to keep from being smelled by animals at a distance, but when you're within 50 yards of a deer or closer, I question whether any efforts along these lines will help. At that range a deer can smell the tiniest off-aroma.

That's why planning your stalk with the wind in mind is so important. The only sure solution is to stay downwind. As you move in close, you must monitor the vagaries of wind closely and be ready to switch to plan B if plan A doesn't seem right. I can feel the slight breeze in my beard, but some hunters tie a light thread to their bow or flick on a butane lighter to test the wind. You can also filter fine dust through your fingers to gauge the lightest breeze.

I think you have to be careful not to get too close to a deer. The wind might seem to be in your favor, but it could be swirling. If you watch smoke from a campfire, you'll see it swirl and go straight up or down where trees or rocks create eddies. A cliff or tree could do the same with your scent, and if you get too close, a deer lying in an eddy could smell you.

If you begin a stalk and find bad wind, back off. That deer will smell you, and he'll be much harder to find and stalk in the future. Leave him alone until conditions are right.

SIGHT

On one of my first stalking attempts, I was crawling toward three bedded bucks when my knee crunched some dry sage leaves. One of the bucks slowly rose from his bed to check out the sound. I was wearing camouflage coveralls, but I wore no hat to cover my blond hair, and my face wasn't camouflaged. It took that buck one millisecond to spot me lying flat at 50 yards, and he and his buddies came uncorked.

CAMOUFLAGE. Since that experience, full camo has saved my bacon many times, and anymore I believe in total camouflage — hat, face, hands, clothes, bow, arrows, shoes, eyeballs, teeth. An experience in Nevada was typical. I saw a buck feeding on one side of a hill, so I approached from the other side. I sneaked in slowly and finally saw his antlers just over the top. He was feeding toward me.

I was standing in the middle of a shale slide, fully exposed with no cover, but it was too late now. I couldn't move. The buck walked to the top of the hill, 30 yards away. Several times he looked directly at me, but it was like he was looking through, not at, me. I froze for 10 minutes as he fed by and when he finally put his head down behind a bush, I slowly drew my bow and put an arrow through his chest. He ran 100 yards and folded. Without camouflage, especially on my face, that buck would have

A lot of hunters wear camouflage clothes but do nothing with their faces. A lot of sense that makes. Unless you have dark skin, the first thing a deer will notice is your white face. As this photo shows, I may be ugly, but at least the deer won't see me.

seen me, no question about it.

Sure, in many cases you can get by without. Cal Coziah, in his book *BUCKS, BOWS AND CAMPFIRES*, bluntly says he doesn't believe in

In low sage like this, I get down and crawl. With three points — two knees and one hand — on the ground all the time I'll never lose my balance, and if a buck hears me and stands up to investigate, he won't see me hidden in the brush.

camouflage. No one can argue with his success, and many other successful bowhunters never use camouflage. Still, that doesn't mean it doesn't help. If camo makes a difference in only one case out of 100, it's worth the trouble to me. I work too hard at getting within bow range to take any chances.

Camouflage clothing has become a fetish, but any dull clothing that blends with the rocks and trees will do. The camo pattern may do some good, but really it's the hue that counts. I'm personally more concerned about the quietness of the material than the pattern.

Actually, I think your face and hands are more critical than your body. Dull clothing means nothing if you leave your white, bald face hanging out. As you stalk, your body will be concealed by brush or other cover anyway, but your face is always exposed, and unless you're dark skinned, it's the shiniest, lightest, most obvious part. Wearing a camouflage shirt and leaving your face white makes as much sense as buying new shoes and going barefoot.

Hands are just as important. As you shoot, your hands must move, and movement will instantly catch a deer's eye. And an animal is a lot more likely to catch the movement of white hands than dark, camouflaged hands. I personally wear green wool gloves as camouflage, because camo cream gets wiped off too fast. In the hot desert you might prefer lightweight mosquito-net gloves.

Tackle and other gear should be camouflaged, too. That's particularly important in desert hunting under direct sunlight. Many times I've spotted hunters from a half-mile or more only because of the signal-mirror flashing of their shiny bows and arrows. Spray your bow with flat paint, and use dull-colored arrows. I like Easton's aluminum arrows anodized into a camouflage pattern.

MOVEMENT. You can be camouflaged from head to toe, but if you move quickly in sight of a buck, you'll get had. You have to move slow. Picture the hands on a clock. You can watch them intently and never see them move, but after awhile they've changed position.

To emphasize this point, I have to go back to Cal Coziah. Even though he spurns camouflage he gets many close shots because he moves SLOW. In *OUTDOOR LIFE* (August 1982), Dewey Haeder wrote:

"Coziah has elevated slow movement to the level of an art. While he covers nonproductive areas at a fast walk, he slows considerably when he gets into gamey country. Frequently, he sits and waits, so inconspicuous that he almost becomes a part of his surroundings."

That's the secret — moving so slow you become part of the surroundings.

COVER. And, of course, use cover to your advantage. First of all, stay off the skyline. Even bushes or trees between you and a buck won't help if you're silhouetted against the sky. In Utah I snuck up on Old Blue, a big gray 4-point. He was feeding in a shallow basin. A little manzanita bush grew at the edge of the basin, so I crawled up behind the bush for cover and peeked over. As soon as my head cleared the edge, Old Blue instantly looked up at me and took off before I could shoot.

"Now how'd he see me behind that bush?" I wondered. To find out I walked down to his position. Looking back up I could see it was obvious I'd been silhouetted against the bright sky, even with the bush for cover. Stay off the skyline.

Don't expect to line up a tree between you and a buck and just walk up on him. It won't work. He'll see you moving. Use solid cover — rocks, hills or other terrain features.

If a buck is bedded under a cliff, you might be able to walk up on him without any special effort, but if he's bedded out in open sage, don't just crouch and try to walk up on him. Not that he'll see you as long as he's bedded. He probably won't. But if he happens to stand up, watch out. A friend of mine was stalking two bedded bucks out in the sage, and he was doing fine just by walking slowly. At least he was until one of the deer stood up. It saw him instantly and took off. In flat country, stay below the brush tops. Crawl. Then even if the buck hears you and gets up to investigate, he won't see you hidden in the brush.

HEARING

I personally don't give deer credit for really great eyes and think you can foil their eyesight pretty easily. Maybe that's because humans have eyes comparable to that of a deer and can relate to a deer's eyesight. What a deer sees, you can see, and with binoculars, you can see even better.

Hearing — along with smell — is a different matter. A deer can detect tiny sounds a person can never hear. As you get close to a buck, you can see his ears swiveling this way and that like radar dishes. I don't have any absolute figures on a deer's hearing ability, but I've seen it demonstrated many times. One time I crawled toward a big buck and was doing great until, right at 35 yards, my ankle popped. That deer jumped up like he'd been rifle-shot. It's hard for us humans to relate to sensitivity like that because we can't experience it, but rest assured, if you make a sound, any buck within 50 yards will hear it.

GO SLOW. Here again, slow motion is the secret. You can't move fast and quiet, but even on bad stuff you can if you go slow enough. Dried sagebrush leaves are worse than Rice Krispies, yet I've crawled across 200 yards of the stuff and got close to deer. It's just a matter of easing your knees and hands into the leaves rather than crunching them.

Shale rock may be even worse, yet again you can get through rock slides without making deer-spooking noises. A few years ago, Rich LaRocco and I sat in the Coast Range of California and watched a blacktail buck lie down under a pine tree in the middle of an open south slope. Rich wanted to try for this buck, but he'd done little stalking and was skeptical.

"You can do it, Rich," I said. "Just take your time and you'll get within range of that buck. Guaranteed!"

"Well, okay," he said with obvious doubt as he ambled off.

Okay, so I look a little strange out here running around in sock feet, but that doesn't bother me because this is the way to kill deer. Shedding your boots and proceeding in sock feet — like a cat — is the biggest single step you can take toward guaranteed stalking.

When he returned to camp that night, he was ecstatic. "You wouldn't believe what happened," he babbled. "I did just what you said and went real slow. I even had to cross a rock slide right behind the buck, but I just moved a rock at a time to get good footing. The stalk took 5 hours but I got within 10 yards of that buck. I couldn't believe it. He was just lying there without a care in the world!"

SOCK FEET. Here's the single most important move you can make to foil a deer's ears — shed your boots. Sure some hunters will say I'm crazy because they've stalked in boots and made it work, but I'll stick my neck out and say you can't stalk worth beans in boots. Sock feet is the only way. Before you say "Hogwash!" try it. You won't need any more convincing from me.

Some hunters substitute running shoes or moccasins for boots, and certainly those are better, but still they can't hold a prayer against sock feet. Even under soft moccasins, gravel will grate together and dried leaves will crackle. But not so with socks. The soft wool molds around the gravel to prevent gritting, and it absorbs the sounds of crushing leaves.

You also can feel the ground. Even the lightest-soled shoes dull your sense of touch, but with sock feet you can detect every rock and twig and literally feel your way without looking at the ground. Socks give you feet like a cat, the ultimate stalking machine.

That brings up one last argument for socks. Moving carelessly in socks, you'll bruise or stab your feet for sure. To keep from hurting yourself, you must move slowly and carefully. Come to think of it, that could be the best reason for stalking in sock feet.

Another skeptical-friend story helps emphasize the point about socks. I'd been telling Mike Cupell that sock feet were the ONLY way, and he so much as said I was goofy. But when he spotted a buck lying at the bottom of a rock slide, and realized he'd never get close grinding through those rocks with his boots, he tried the sock trick.

"Dwight, I just couldn't believe how much difference sock feet made," he later told me. "I walked within 15 yards of that buck. It was neat."

You probably wear heavy socks for hiking, so you can just slip off your boots and start stalking. That's fine, but to save my good socks, I carry a pair of old socks to slip on for stalking. These should be dark to blend with the ground. One time I saw a buck lying 100 yards downhill in a clump of junipers, and to reach him I had to cross a long stretch of open gravel, a must situation for socks. I'd forgot my stalking socks and was wearing new white socks, which the deer would spot right off. So I took off my green T-shirt and ripped it in half and wrapped it around my feet. Two hours later I stood within 10 yards of that buck as he dozed contentedly in the shade. T-shirt or socks, it doesn't matter. Just get rid of those boots.

THE THREE-POINT SYSTEM. One other principle helps in quiet movement, and that's balance. If you just try walking along, you'll constantly lose your balance and dance around to keep from crashing. Sooner or later you'll make some noise and get caught.

To avoid that, employ what I call the tripod effect. Keep at least three points on the ground. Wherever it's feasible, get down and crawl (knee pads can help save your knees in gravel). That way you have your knees and at least one hand on the ground to form a stable tripod that won't tip. In a situation where I can stalk by crouching, I always keep one hand on the ground to form a tripod with my legs.

In steep country where it's impossible to crawl downhill, I sit facing down. With my heels, rear end, and one hand — my bow is in the other hand — as contact points on the ground, I can keep three points on the ground and crab-walk downhill toward a buck and never lose my balance.

That pretty well covers the mechanics of stalking. If you apply them, I guarantee you'll get close to more than 80 percent of the deer you stalk.

CURIOSITY

A deer's smell, sight and hearing are the major senses you must contend with in stalking, but deer have one other sense — or maybe trait would be a more accurate word — that often enters into the outcome of a hunt. That's curiosity. This one, however, works for you.

No matter how skilled you get at stalking, it's tough to get through a buck's radar field infallibly, and eventually you'll get caught. That buck will hear or see you, and he'll nail you to the wall.

A natural reaction at that moment is to draw and shoot fast before he takes off. Don't waste your arrow. The chances of making a good hit on a tense buck looking at you are slim and none. You often hear about deer "jumping the string," and it probably happens most often in this situation. I personally think calm, undisturbed bucks rarely if ever jump the string, but alert bucks will do it frequently. In fact, I'm convinced a deer can react fast enough to dodge an arrow if he sees it coming. Debate that if you will, but first try shooting at a few alert bucks. You probably won't get to full draw on most of them, and you'll miss most of the others because they'll be gone before your arrow gets there.

So what's the alternative? Be cool. It has been a rare stalk during which I haven't been caught off guard. Dozens of times bucks have either heard or seen me. You'd think that would end the stalk, but that's where the curiosity factor takes over. As I've said, a buck doesn't need a second opinion if he smells you. He just splits. But if he only hears or sees you, he'll investigate. He's curious. And if he can't find further cause for alarm, he'll forget about you.

The buck that jumped up when my ankle popped is a good example. He had me dead to rights, but because I was crawling low in the sage, all he could see was my head and face — which were camouflaged. He stared a full 5 minutes, but when he didn't see or hear any more suspicious doings, he started feeding and gave me a perfect shot at 30 yards. Which I missed. Nice going.

One August I was photographing deer at Steens Mountain in Oregon. I'd crawled within 40 yards of a bedded buck and slowly eased my camera over a rock to shoot some pictures. The buck saw the camera and stood up. He took a few cautious steps toward me and peered for several minutes. He'd caught me in an awkward position, and I was about ready to scream out with muscle cramps when he finally decided a camera on a rock was no big deal and started scratching his back and then turned to walk away. He went only 20 yards and lay down just beyond a big rock. That's typical. Deer seem to think, "Out of sight, out of mind," and they'll often bed again just as close, but where they can't see you. I proceeded to stalk even closer to this buck in his second bed.

In badlands country north of Miles City, Montana, I watched three bucks — two forked horns and a small 4-point — bed in a shallow wash. I circled around to come in from the back side and crawled toward the top of the wash. It seemed like a cinch, but little did I know one of the forked horns had got up and bedded on a bank above the wash. I stuck my head over a little rise and there he was, looking right at me. He cocked his ears curiously and slowly stood up.

He had me. The grass here was knee-high to a worm, and all I could do was lie flat and hope. He pranced back and forth and then, with his ears laid back, walked stiff legged into the wash with the other bucks. I expected to see them all strutting suspiciously out the other side, but after 10 minutes they hadn't showed. So I crawled to the edge, and there were all

As I eased my camera and 400mm lens over a rock, this buck spotted the movement instantly. I froze and the deer stared for five minutes and even took a few steps toward me.

But when he could detect no further movement or sound, he forgot about me and started scratching his back, and then he walked about 20 yards and bedded down again. Out of sight, out of mind. When a buck catches you off guard, don't give up!

three bucks, feeding peacefully, all within 15 yards. I nailed one of the forked horns.

I've seen that happen time and time again. Unless deer catch you walking around in plain sight, or smell you, they'll display more curiosity than fright, so even when things look desperate, don't start flinging desperate arrows. Play it cool. You'll get the shot you want if you hang tough. Don't give up!

PUTTING IT ALL TOGETHER

This all sounds well and good, but does it really work? Many years ago I'd devised grand stalking schemes in my mind and had even pulled off a few stalks and taken a couple of deer, but I still had doubts about the overall application of this system. Sure it worked in easy places, but what about the tough spots? It seemed stalking a deer would be impossible in some cases, and unless a hunting method had universal application, it had to be considered weak.

Then came my chance to test stalking to the Nth degree. Dave Hummel and I sat on a desert rimrock in Oregon, and just at sunrise we spotted two bucks, a large 3-point and a smaller 4-point, feeding near the bottom of a canyon a half-mile away. They fed and shoved each other around for awhile, and then at 8:30 a.m. they bedded under a juniper tree right in the middle of a canyon wall.

Their side was barren except for the bedding tree. The 150 yards from the deer to the top of the rim was wide open shale and gravel. A stalk looked impossible, but I've always figured you can't do something if you don't try, so through a spotting scope I studied the slope above the bucks. In places, big rocks seemed to offer possible footing in the loose gravel, and little dirt chutes that might offer quiet footing down through the rocks. Just above the bucks, at 30 yards, grew a scrub juniper 3 feet high. I pictured myself crouched behind that bush, ready to shoot.

"Guess I'll give 'em a try," I said to Dave.

"You're nuts," he said tactfully. "You'll never get close."

"Yep. Thirty yards. Easy!"

"Bull!"

What choice had he given me? Nobody could pass up a challenge like that. Now it was do or die.

For another hour I studied every detail of the terrain above the deer to plan my route. By 10 o'clock warming air was blowing steadily uphill to give me reliable wind, so I set out to circle the head of the canyon to the bucks' side. Dave stayed put to watch.

From the rim above the deer, I could just see the tips of antlers under the tree. At least they were still there, but things looked tough now. I took off my boots and left them on top, and started down toward the bucks, stepping from one big rock to another.

A half-hour later, 50 yards down the hill, I came over a little rise and could see the 3-point in clear view, lying at the edge of the tree's shade. He faced downhill, but the side of his face was visible, so he would be able to see me out the corner of his eye. Rock hopping was out now. The slope was too steep for crawling downward, so I sat down and slowly crab-walked toward the bucks, moving only slightly, then stopping to watch.

I'd covered 25 yards and was sitting in the open when the 3-point stood up. He turned to face me and stared. "Oh, no," I thought. "That's the end of this stalk." I thought about drawing slowly to shoot, but with me in plain view that would never work. I froze. The buck stared for 5 minutes. Apparently satisfied that he'd seen nothing, he walked uphill and lay down behind the tree trunk where he couldn't see me. Out of sight, out of mind.

Now the deer were within 75 yards, critical hearing range, and they'd hear even the slightest sound. By placing my heels solidly in the rocks and putting a hand on the ground behind my back, then lifting my rear and setting it farther down the hill, I used the tripod principle to perfection. And feeling the ground with my sock feet, I didn't have to look each step for solid footing and could keep an eye on the 4-point's ears to tell instantly if he'd heard me. Several times his ears snapped to attention as if he were listening, and each time I froze and waited until he relaxed. He never got up.

My progress was slow but steady, and finally, right at 1 p.m., crouched behind the scrub juniper just above the bucks, I became part of the picture exactly as I'd visualized it 3 hours earlier from the far side of the canyon. I'd achieved my goal with only one difference — the distance was 25 yards, not 30. The bucks lay calmly, looking out over the canyon, and I nocked an arrow, poised to shoot.

It was a great triumph. Whether I made the shot seemed insignificant now. The stalk had worked, the system was valid. Dave had seen it and needed no further proof. Still I had to rub it in. Just a little.

"Bull!" I whispered, hoping the bucks wouldn't hear me.

CHAPTER 8

THE SHOT

Getting within 25 yards of a buck should guarantee venison in camp, and I'd like to report a perfect ending to that perfect stalk, as Dave Hummel watched, but it just didn't happen.

The sun was intense that day, and after an hour of sitting still and waiting for one of the bucks to get up, I felt well broiled on one side and turned to let the other side cook for awhile. My foot hit some rocks, which rolled down the hill, and the 4-point jumped up and glared at me. I held still because he couldn't see me, but as soon as he looked away I impulsively drew and shot. The arrow flew just over the buck's back. With the shot, both deer bounded down the canyon. A long cobweb glistening in the sunlight trailed from the smaller buck's antlers, waving goodbye.

A lot of hunts end just that way — everything goes perfect until that arrow is released. My question is: What good is spotting lots of deer and stalking within bow range if you blow it in the end? The obvious answer is: No good at all. If you can't bring the hunt to a successful conclusion — that is, kill the deer — then all the great hunting ability in the world means nothing. You've got to make that shot or you're not a complete hunter.

DEFINING THE SHOT

Clark Unruh, a farmer in southern Oregon, started hunting Hart Mountain and the Malheur National Wildlife Refuge in eastern Oregon back in the 1950s when few hunters in that part of the world had ever seen a bow and arrow.

"If we'd known how to hunt back then, we could have taken 30-inch bucks every year," Unruh said. "It was incredible, but I never killed a deer in those early days."

Since then the quality of deer herds in these desert units, and in particular the size of the bucks, has fallen off considerably, yet in recent years, with tougher hunting, Unruh has taken several tremendous bucks. He thinks that's because he's learned the difference between getting shots and getting a good shot.

"We used to leave camp in the morning with back quivers packed with 2 or 3 dozen arrows," he related. "We'd keep going hard and shooting at every deer we saw. We'd return to camp at night with empty quivers.

"That's why we never got anything. With experience I've learned that the number of deer you see and the quantity of shots you get isn't necessarily what gets you a deer. It's far more important to get ONE good shot."

THE GOOD SHOT. That should be your goal — to get ONE good shot. If you operate under the philosophy of quantity, you'll shoot lots of arrows and kill few deer.

It's hard to define a "good shot" because it depends so much on your ability, but a few ideas might help. In whitetail hunting from a stand, you might be able to guarantee 20 yard shots, but that's not true in open-country hunting. As I've said you can get within 50 yards of virtually any buck, but 20? Sometimes yes, sometimes no. To assure yourself of a good chance at a mule deer, learn to shoot well out to 50 yards and you'll be in the ballpark.

Most hunters who use compound bows aim with sights and shoot very deliberately. If you practice that way then you should go for comparable shots in the field. You can't practice standing flatfooted and carefully going through each step at the target butt, and then suddenly expect to make an instinctive running shot in the field.

One writer said the longbow is far better for running shots than a compound. I agree, it probably is, but I disagree with the basic assumption — that you must shoot at running deer. In my opinion, the whole idea is to get an unhurried shot at a stationary deer. If you have to shoot at a running deer, you blew the stalk in the first place.

For most hunters, regardless of tackle, running shots are pure folly. I realize many stick-bow shooters will say I'm nuts, and that's fine. If you practice running shots regularly maybe you feel confident with them. Some friends of mine have developed a machine that throws milk cartons and sponge-rubber footballs into the air, and they practice shooting at these with their long bows. They've gotten so they can regularly nail flying targets. Other hunters practice shooting thrown frisbees, and some roll old tires down hills and shoot at them for running target practice. If you practice this way, and can make these shots consistently, then far be it from me to tell you not to shoot at running deer.

TEST YOURSELF. The important thing is to know what you can do

Test yourself to gauge your ability. If you can't make a shot in practice, then you can't expect to make it in the field on deer. Find out how far away you can keep arrows in a paper
plate and you'll know about how far you can shoot with confidence at deer.

and go for a shot within your abilities. For me personally that means a
standing, motionless deer no farther than 50 yards away. Based on my
ability, any stationary deer within that range presents a good shot.

That might not be true for you, of course. Maybe you can shoot farther, or maybe you don't feel confident past 30 yards. Test yourself to gauge your ability. Cliff Dewell, who has killed a number of mule deer and blacktails, offers one method of testing yourself.

"The kill area on an average buck is about the size of a 12-inch paper plate," Dewell said. "Put up a paper plate and shoot at it from various unmarked yardages and different positions to find out at what distance you can keep your arrows in that plate. That's your deer-shooting range."

That's a good concept, because it offers a way to determine your truly effective range. If it turns out to be 80 yards stationary, fine. If it's 80 yards running, fine. But if it's 30 yards or closer, stationary, be honest enough to admit it, and go for that shot in the field. My definition of a good shot is one you're sure you can make. The object of stalking is not to shoot an arrow, it's to get a good shot. One you can make. Don't settle for anything less.

GETTING THE SHOT

There comes a moment in any successful stalk when you suddenly realize you're going to get the shot. For me it's not a rational thing. I don't calmly say to myself, "Dwight, old fellow, you're going to get a shot, by cracky."

Actually it comes by taste and feel. I get this terrible cow-manure taste in my mouth and my palms begin to sweat icewater, and freezing drops of sweat pour from my arm pits and dribble down my sides, and along with that comes an unrelenting urge to rush. To get it over with fast. When these sensations start building up in me, I know the moment of truth has arrived. You probably won't have the same reactions, but whatever the signs, when you sense a shot coming on, remember a few important steps. What you do in these critical moments will determine whether you get the good shot. Or blow it.

CONTROL. Maybe this one word sums up this whole business of stalking. Getting close to a buck is like any other strong emotional experience, like a violent argument or falling in love. When emotions replace reason, you very easily can lose control. It's one thing to watch a buck from a quarter-mile away and calmly picture yourself crawling up behind a bush 20 yards from the buck and nocking an arrow and aiming just like you do on the target range and smoothly releasing that arrow. Emotionally it's totally different when you're there. Your heart sounds like someone's chopping wood, and your knees feel like water balloons, and you're overwhelmed with a violent urge to jump up and shoot an arrow now!

Get ahold of yourself, man (or woman). This is no time to let your emotions run rampant. If ever there were a time to maintain control, to move slowly and deliberately, now is the time. That's the only way you'll get a good shot. If you allow yourself to make one hurried, careless move, you'll end up with one of those running shots you've never practiced.

Control yourself.

STAY BACK. The essence of stalking, of course, is getting close to animals. If that weren't the case, you just as well hunt with a rifle. For a couple of reasons, however, I think you can get too close.

First, the margin of error is so small at ultra-close range — 25 yards and less — you can't afford even the slightest mistake. It's true, you can get caught in the act of stalking — either the buck sees or hears you — and as long as you play it cool, you'll get by. But that principle deserves a corollary: The closer you are, the more critical it becomes. At 100 yards a deer can spot your head moving through the sage, and he'll forget you if you freeze. At 30 yards, he might hear you snap a twig, and if he can't pick up any more foul play, he'll settle down. But if he senses even the slightest disturbance closer than that, chances are he'll explode without further ado.

I've talked to dozens of hunters about stalking deer, and many express discouragement because the deer always come boiling out of their beds in a cloud of dust and present no chance for a good shot. In most cases these hunters have just tried to get too close. Even after they're within good range, they keep pushing on, forcing their hand, trying to see the buck lying in its bed. If a buck spots you that close, he'll come out cooking. Get within good range and stop. (I'll say more about what to do next in a little while.)

Second, when you get close to a buck, the tension becomes almost oppressive. The air seems full of electricity; you can almost feel the vibrations of the buck's radar pulsing through your nervous system. You have to possess cast-iron nerves to control yourself under that pressure, to make yourself pick a spot, to draw slowly and smoothly, to aim carefully before casting an arrow. At a distance of 40 yards from a buck, I can stay fairly calm and shoot deliberately; at 20 yards the presence of that buck is so overpowering I virtually black out and forget to aim. I've missed far more deer by getting too close and losing my head than I have by making bad shots from longer range.

Consider what happened in Idaho. One morning I had a perfect broadside shot at a big whitetail buck. I could see him coming and was ready as he stepped into an opening at 20 yards. He gave me a perfect shot, but my mind nearly went blank and I shot a terrible arrow.

The next day I saw an equally fine buck walking down a fire road, 60 yards away. At that range I knew he wouldn't see, hear or smell me. The electricity of the close-range encounter was absent. This was just a deer down the hill, not unlike a target on a hay bale. I deliberately drew an arrow, aimed carefully, released smoothly and followed through, just as I'd done hundreds of times on the practice range. The arrow sailed into space and curved into that buck's chest like a bowling ball hooking into the strike pocket. The deer trotted 30 yards and fell over dead.

BE PATIENT. Impatience undoubtedly has kept many of us from getting good shots. It has certainly foiled me a few times. One time I slipped within 30 yards of a buck bedded under a juniper tree. I feel absolutely confident of my shooting ability at 30 yards, so that seemed plenty close enough and I sat down to wait for the buck to get up and give me a shot. The wind was strong and steady in my favor so he wouldn't smell me. It was simply a matter of time. If I waited patiently, he'd eventually be a dead buck.

But after an hour he still hadn't stirred, and I got impatient. Just downhill, a couple of bushes would give me cover. If I could just crawl up behind them, I could probably shoot him right in his bed....

A half-hour later I stood within 10 yards of the buck, he on one side of a tree, I on the other. Slowly I peeked around the trunk to look for a shooting hole and instantly he spotted my head and boiled out from under that tree like a scalded cat.

"If only I'd waited," I moaned. "Why did I have to get so close?"

WAIT HIM OUT. I recommend you stalk within good shooting range and then, if conditions are right, find yourself a comfortable place to sit, and settle in. Don't try to get any closer, and don't try to make the deer get up. Bide your time until he gets up to feed or stretch on his own. Deer normally move around during the day, so with time he'll present the shot you want.

Why wait? Because he'll get up calm. He'll feed peacefully and keep his head buried in the brush for long periods, giving you time to draw unseen, and he'll turn one way and then another slowly to present just the right shooting angle. With patience, you can get the perfect shot at just the buck you want. And that's the whole idea behind bowhunting.

OTHER APPROACHES. That's the ideal, but it won't always work. With any shifting of the wind, you know the buck will smell you. I recall one time waiting too patiently and blowing the whole thing as a result. I'd spotted two high-mountain bucks feeding in a snowbrush patch. By the time I got close they'd bedded, and by now a blustery storm was brewing. I crawled through the brush and got within 30 yards of the bucks, but they were both screened by branches and presented no shot, so even though the wind was unstable, I sat down to wait. That was a mistake. About 10 minutes later, the wind whipped from behind me toward the deer, and instantly they scrambled from their beds and tore off down the mountain.

Sometimes other deer may be wandering around and could give you away, or in some cases I've just got so darned sunbaked and thirsty sitting there I couldn't hack it any longer and had to go for a shot right away.

ROCK THROW. So how to you get a buck to stand up and give you a shot? Tossing rocks is one way, and it works pretty well because it diverts the deer's attention from you.

One morning I spotted a nice 3x4 buck feeding in high sage. At 9 a.m. he lay down totally hidden, but a clump of yellow rabbitbrush pretty well marked his position. I stalked within 20 yards of him and sat down to wait, but the wind was bad, so I decided to throw some rocks to get him up.

I threw a pebble to the side. Nothing happened. Another pebble.

Nothing. A third, this time closer. It made a distinct crunch, and slowly the old buck rose out of his bed. It had worked perfectly except for one thing — the buck was only about half as far as I'd thought. When he stood up at 10 yards, my heart shifted into high. But he was looking straight away at the rock I'd actually thrown OVER him, and he presented a perfect shot.

Be careful to move your arm as little as possible so your clothes don't swish or the deer will stand up looking at you rather than the rock. Also, be sure you throw accurately. Late one morning I crawled up behind a 3-point lying on a sagebrush point. Again the wind was undependable, so I pitched a couple of rocks. The buck didn't hear them so I tried to get one a little closer, but this one got hung up in my finger tab and nearly beaned the buck. He leaped up and tore off down the hill before I could shoot.

CALLING. I've also had good success by bleating softly on a predator call. The problem is the deer will get up to look at you, so you must hide. When he can't see anything unusual, he'll lose interest and start feeding. That's when you ease up for a shot.

MAKING THE SHOT

Getting a good shot, and MAKING that shot aren't necessarily the same thing. As you can tell from some of my stories, I've proved that many times, and many conversations with other bowhunters show I'm not alone. It's easy to blow a good shot if you're not prepared.

BEFORE THE HUNT. Making a shot starts long before you ever get close to a deer. Chuck Adams, a well-know bowhunter and writer, is one of the deadliest game shots around, so I asked him what he does to make sure he connects at the critical moment.

"I think it all starts with well-tuned equipment," Chuck said. "I spend hours matching arrows and broadheads to my bows, and sighting in to make sure everything is just right. If your tackle is perfectly tuned, you'll have confidence when the time comes to shoot at game. If it's not, you'll have doubts. You must have confidence to make the shots that count."

FORM. Along with that I think goes good shooting form. Missing a shot because you get nervous is one thing, but missing regularly because you're simply a lousy shot is another. Traditional archers decry the compound bow because it supposedly has made everyone an instant success, but that's not true. I know lots of bowhunters who can't hit a target half the time at 25 yards, let alone a deer, because they've never learned shooting fundamentals. They just go hunting and start flinging arrows, their gear unmatched, their release rough, no follow through. One fellow had been "bowhunting" for several years and didn't even know he was supposed to use the same anchor point each shot. He just pulled the string back to his ear and let her fly.

The scope of this book doesn't cover shooting basics, but let's just say good form is the starting point for all good shooting. If possible take a lesson or two from a qualified instructor and it will save you from years of

Unquestionably, bowhunters miss more deer because they fail to pick a spot than for any other reason. Since a deer doesn't have a built in bullseye, you have create your own visually. Before you shoot, pick a spot! (Photo by Pat Miller.)

struggling with bad shooting habits. If you can't take lessons, at least study books or magazine articles to get tips on good form. (See Appendix B for a guide to basic shooting. If you develop the good habits outlined here, you can't go wrong.)

PRACTICE UNDER PRESSURE. Harold Boyack has a trophy-buck record equaled by few other hunters. A number of his mule deer appear in the Pope and Young Record book, including the No. 3 nontypical. To kill bucks like that, Boyack has to maintain control under pressure.

"Shooting in tournaments has helped my hunting," Boyack said. "Even if you don't care about winning trophies, shooting in front of your peers puts you in a stress situation, much the same way hunting does, so it's really good for mind control. That's what you have to have to kill big bucks."

FIELD PRACTICE. Another vital step, Boyack thinks, is stump shooting, or roving, as many hunters call it. He walks through the field, shooting at pine cones, stumps, dirt banks, cow pies — any convenient target at various ranges.

"Roving is the ultimate practice for bowhunters," Boyack said. "It trains you for the kind of shooting you'll do while hunting."

While roving shoot from the various positions — kneeling, crouched — you might encounter while stalking. Rarely can you shoot at a deer from the comfortable, relaxed, standing positions you use when you're shooting at targets.

Also, be sure you shoot uphill and downhill a lot. Most western deer country is very steep, and you often have to shoot at sharp angles. If you aim for the actual distance from you to a deer you'll shoot high, especially on downhill shots, so practice these to learn how much to hold under.

Oregon bowhunter Chuck Warner has specialized in mule deer hunting, and his record shows he has mastered the art. He has killed two typical mule deer that score higher than 170 and a non-typical that scores 185, and he's taken many smaller bucks most of us would crawl across a bed of nails to shoot.

Warner thinks familiarity with your equipment is the starting point. "You have to practice enough before the seasons that shooting becomes automatic," Warner said. "If you have to think about shooting and aiming during the heat of the action, you'll blow the shot."

But Warner also emphasizes the need for practice during the hunt. "I always carry a practice arrow with a Judo or blunt head in my quiver," Warner said. "During any hunt I shoot constantly along the trail to and from camp at pine cones and stumps so that when the time comes to shoot a buck, my muscles are loose and my eye is sharp. I think this constant practice as you're hunting is very important."

PICKING A SPOT. The advice you hear most commonly is to "pick a spot." It's been said so much it has become a cliche, but that doesn't take away from its truth. Deer don't come with a built-in aiming point, so you have to imagine one when you're shooting. Aiming generally at the whole deer, rather than at one particular point on that deer, has probably been responsible for more misses than any other single point.

Clark Unruh, who has killed many fine bucks with his bow, said he thinks the attitude you have when you get ready to shoot is what makes a difference. You have to be thinking clearly to pick a spot.

"Back in the early days we just shot arrows. Standing in one spot, I missed seven different bucks as they filed past single file within easy bow range. I was just shooting at the whole deer. You have to pick one small spot on that deer. I clearly remember the first deer I ever killed at Hart Mountain," Unruh said. "The sun was shining on him and I remember picking the exact hair I was going to shoot at. I think I split that hair."

Harold Boyack agrees that shooting at a whole deer may be the No. 1 bowhunter's sin.

"I had a young friend who could nail ground squirrels out to 40 and 50 yards," Boyack said. "But he had a terrible time on big game. One day he missed a bull elk broadside at 25 yards, right out in the open. 'Harold,' he said, 'three of my sight pins were on that bull, and I knew one of them had to be right. That arrow had to hit him.' But he missed that elk.

"Finally I told him, 'You're not picking a spot. Next time, visualize a ground squirrel on a deer's chest and shoot at that squirrel.' The guy did just that and he killed the next buck he shot at."

If visualizing ground squirrels doesn't work for you, try taping a reminder to your bow. On one bow I had a piece of tape that said:

A small printed reminder on the face of a bow limb, right where you'll see it before you shoot, can help you focus on the important parts of making a shot.

1. Pick a spot.
2. Count three seconds.
3. Follow through.

Before shooting at a deer, I read that tape to focus my mind on the important steps. (The "count three seconds" reminded me to take time to aim, because I'd got in the habit of shooting too fast.) At any rate, I distinctly remember going through those steps on one deer. I first saw him at 40 yards, bedded under a cliff. He was looking out over the valley without a care in the world. I read the sign on my bow and then looked at the deer and said to myself, "I'm going to hit that tuft of hair just behind his front shoulder." I drew and aimed, held for a good 3 seconds, and released. The arrow hit within a couple of inches of my aiming point, and I got the buck.

Cliff Dewell, an excellent bowhunter, has a similar sign on his bow. It reads, "Stay calm, Pick a spot."

"Just glancing at that before I shoot helps me think about what I'm doing," Dewell said.

(The subject of shot placement is discussed further in the Chapter 9, "After the Shot.")

PRACTICE ON THE REAL THING. One day as I walked down a dirt road, a bowhunter driving by stopped to give me a ride, and as usual I asked, "How are you doing?"

"Well, I've never killed a deer with a bow," he said. "But then I'm trophy hunting. I won't shoot anything but a big one."

"How many years you been bowhunting?" I asked.

"Twelve," he said.

At the time I admired his dedication, but now I think he was defeating himself. He would be lucky ever to kill a trophy, even if he got a good shot.

You can't learn to shoot animals by dreaming about it. I think a person who starts right out as a "trophy hunter" makes a mistake because he's left out the vital first step of experience. You've got to pay your dues to mature as a bowhunter. If you've shot lots of game with a rifle, then you might start right out bowhunting with confidence. But if you're a beginning hunter, you'll do yourself a favor by taking a few animals, even if they're does or small bucks, to gain confidence and discipline.

Practice on animals may be the only way to truly develop spot-picking ability, but unfortunately, few of us can legally shoot enough to deer to develop our skills fully, so we have to look to other kinds of game for additional experience. Chuck Adams said he credits part of his success to the fact that he shoots year-around and takes every opportunity he can to hunt game. He hunts feral hogs and goats regularly, which he thinks has helped him greatly on deer, but when he can't hunt these, he'll shoot ground squirrels, marmots, rabbits and other small game.

"Shooting inanimate targets is a lot different from shooting at animals," he said. "You just can't experience the same feelings on the target range that you do on animals, even small game. To learn to shoot game, you have to shoot game."

I agree. During years when I've had time to hunt small game in the spring, I've done well on deer, but during busy years when work has cut into my off-season hunting, my deer shooting has suffered. Even shooting ground squirrels forces you to judge range, pick a spot, and concentrate much as you have to do in deer hunting.

BE CALM. Finally, maybe the real secret, as Cliff Dewell's bow sticker says, is to stay calm. Dewell said he just tells himself, "Be calm, don't get nervous," and Chuck Warner said the same thing. He just tries to stay calm.

Other hunters go through a routine. Chuck Adams uses reverse psychology on himself.

"If I told myself, 'You're going to get a shot, you can do it,' I'd get so nervous I couldn't hit anything," Adams said. "So instead I tell myself over and over during a stalk, 'This is impossible, it can't be done, you'll never get a shot.' That way I'm not expecting any great results, so when the time comes to shoot, I'm surprised it's happening and I'm relaxed."

Clark Unruh said that perhaps most important of all, once he has decided he's going after a buck, he just forgets about the antlers. If he's picked that deer to shoot, the decisions have all been made. He has no further reason to look at the antlers, so he just looks at the body as a target.

"I do one other thing," Unruh said. "I develop a routine when I'm practicing and I carry it right into the field with me, and go through the same routine on deer I go through on targets. I tip my hat back a little and remember to relax my grip on the bow. Then I pick a spot. That gives me something familiar to work with and calms me down."

CONFIDENCE

Maybe this all boils down to one final concept. Confidence. Fine tuning your bow, building good form, practicing in the field, shooting game — these all have a cumulative effect on your mind, and the end result is confidence.

Without the firm conviction that you really can do it, doubts will infect your actions, and you'll be tentative. You'll choke.

"Lack of confidence is what breeds the shakes," Harold Boyack said. "You must have confidence. Remember, though, it's not an inborn thing. Confidence grows out of constant practice. One time Tom Jennings, the bow designer, and I were hunting together, and after watching me for awhile, he said, 'Harold, when you shoot, you have absolute confidence you're going to hit that animal, don't you?'

"And I guess that's right. I've trained myself for this moment and have shot so much I have total confidence. Let me tell you, after the shot I turn to jelly, but before that arrow flies, I have no doubts."

CHAPTER 9

AFTER THE SHOT

The last weekend of Oregon's bow season a few years back I had only two days to hunt and wanted some venison. Time was short and didn't allow room for error, so I practiced hard and prepared myself mentally to take advantage of any opportunity.

At daylight I started hiking up a high ridge, glassing ahead into openings among scattered clumps of mountain mahogany. Less than a half-hour into day I spotted a forked horn feeding my way, so I maneuvered in front of him and waited with confidence as he came within 40 yards, 30, then 25. No doubts entered my mind as the buck fed slowly by, broadside, head down. I centered the 25-yard sight pin just behind his shoulder, held for several seconds, and let the string slip from my fingers.

As the arrow passed through his chest and rattled off rocks beyond, the buck whirled and disappeared over a rise. I set my gear on the ground and walked down the hill to look for the buck. He lay dead, 50 yards away.

That was strictly a workmanlike hunt with little emotion but much efficiency. My attitude about finding that buck might seem too casual since I didn't wait an hour and search for blood sign before taking up the trail as bowhunters are supposed to do, but with a perfect hit at close range, I had no doubts. The buck was down.

SHOT PLACEMENT

You commonly read that arrows kill by hemorrhage, so you must wait

When my arrow hit this forked horn, there was no doubt in my mind that the animal had gone down quickly. A well placed shot is the secret to recovering deer.

long periods to let an animal bleed out, and then you must track carefully. In many cases, that's true, but it seems to me that view, if left unqualified, misses the point. Indeed, arrows do cause bleeding, which can kill an animal, but that's not how well-placed shots kill. They destroy vital organs. In most cases, a deer with an arrow through his lungs doesn't die from blood loss. His lungs collapse and he suffocates. And a buck shot through the heart doesn't bleed to death. He dies from cardiac arrest. To put it another way, deer hit in the lungs or heart die long before they could bleed to death.

I'm not trying to dispute tradition, only to say that the common view about hemorrhage and trailing ability begs the point — that a well-placed arrow is the real secret to recovering animals. If you hit an animal on the money, you don't have to trail him; you just walk over and start gutting. Most of the bucks I've killed have piled up within 100 yards and have required no trailing at all.

SHOOT FOR THE LUNGS. Some hunters would debate just where to shoot a deer, but I'll go on record as saying the only safe target is the lungs. Hitting the heart kills a deer just as fast, of course, but the heart offers a small target that gives small margin for error, so I think you always should aim for lungs.

One common mistake is shooting too far behind the front leg.

The lungs present the only really good aiming point, and they don't extend far behind the front shoulder. To hit the lungs, shoot at the hair line just behind the front leg, and about one-third to halfway up the chest. (Photo by Pat Miller.)

Sometime when you kill a deer, skin one side and cut out the rib meat to see just where the heart and lungs lie. You'll find the lungs scarcely extend behind the front leg. To hit them on a broadside deer, you want to aim at the hair line just behind the leg, in a straight line above the "elbow."

Shooting this far forward, you might be afraid of hitting the leg bone, but here again, as you skin an animal look at the front leg and you'll discover the leg bone angles forward from the elbow to form a "V". Shooting at the hair line behind the front leg gives you plenty of clearance. If you shoot back a little too far you'll hit the liver, which will bring down a deer fairly quickly, but if you hit behind the liver, you'll hit paunch, and then you've got problems.

Aim for a spot one-third to half way up the chest but no higher. If you shoot too high, you'll hit only an empty "air space" between the lungs and the backbone and you probably won't recover the deer. On the other hand, if you shoot a little low, you'll hit the heart, which is just as good as hitting lungs.

Broadside shots are okay, but quartering-away shots are better because the arrow passes diagonally through the animal's body and is more sure to catch vital organs. Hold for the same vertical height — one-third to one-half way up the chest — and aim at the front leg on the opposite side. You'll get lungs.

SHOOTING DOWN. These ideas assume you're on the deer's level, but often in steep mule deer country, you'll shoot up or down. Most commonly you'll stalk down on a buck and will shoot downhill, possibly straight down over a cliff. Then you may be shooting at the buck's back, but even that's a good angle as long as your arrow can get to the lungs. Your aiming point will vary greatly, depending on how steep the angle is

I don't recommend this shot. The buck is calm and won't jump the string, but you have little margin for error. Shooting a deer facing straight away is okay if you can shoot down on his back to hit lungs directly, but I don't recommend shooting a deer like this in the rump. He doesn't know you're there, so wait until he presents a better angle.

and the buck's position, but try to shoot so the arrow will angle between the deer's front legs and you'll get lungs or heart.

One book on bowhunting for deer suggests neck shots as feasible when you have no other choice, but I say you have another choice. Not shooting. You could get lucky and hit the jugular vein, but that's risky. Don't shoot at a deer's neck.

HEAD ON. For a buck facing you head on, you can aim for the lower chest and you'll get lungs or heart, and that's not a bad shot, but still I don't recommend head-on shots, especially if the deer sees you and has tensed. He can react the instant you release the string, and you could hit him poorly.

TAIL END. Shooting at a deer facing straight away is okay if you're shooting down onto his back, because your arrow can hit the lungs directly, but I don't recommend shooting a deer in the rump. It's true an arrow through the rump can run body length to reach the lungs and heart. Also, it could cut the femoral artery down the inside of a back leg, which guarantees a quick kill, but the margin of error is small. You could hit the pelvis, or plant an arrow in the meaty ham and do nothing but cripple the deer. If you've stalked well, you'll have time to wait for him to turn, and eventually he'll present a clean side shot.

AFTER THE SHOT

After you've hit an animal, you want to avoid stirring him up any more than necessary. Many deer will streak away wildly after they're hit, but often they'll react calmly, as if nothing has happened, and in that case, hide quietly and watch. I shot one buck back a little too far, through the liver. This buck flinched, and walked away slowly, and several other bucks with him followed along behind. They might have heard the "thunk" of my bow, but they weren't spooked so I stayed hidden and watched. All the bucks wandered slowly away, but after going 50 yards, the one I'd shot stopped and looked back, and he stood there for 10 minutes as if looking for the source of the disturbance. Then he took a couple of wobbly steps and fell over dead.

Anytime you have a deer in sight, stay put and watch. Don't move. The buck probably doesn't even know you're around and, just as my buck did, he may just fall over or lie down, and then you've got him. If a deer runs out of your sight, sprint to the nearest vantage point to watch him. Often in open-country hunting you can see for miles, and you can watch a deer go down, even if he runs a half-mile. I've watched many deer go down.

If he crashes during mid-flight, you know he's dead, but if he just stops running and lies down, stay away until you're sure he's dead. The last thing you want is to spook that buck and start him running again. Even if he's hit vitally, he could run a long way before he stops again, and that just makes finding him all the tougher. Sit and watch until he dies. As long as he's in sight, you've got hope, but if you start him running again, your chances of recovering the buck go down drastically. In some cases, you might be able to sneak in for another shot, but that's risky unless you're sure you can shoot again without spooking him.

In particular take time to mark the buck's position. If he's a long way off, say across a canyon, you might not be able to find him once you get over there. I dwelt at length on the idea of marking a buck under "Planning a Stalk," and the same principles apply here to finding a dead or wounded deer.

If a buck gets out of sight quickly, you should take a different approach. If you're sure of a lung hit, as I was on that forked horn, then you have little reason to wait, but if the hit was questionable, waiting offers the safest choice. Sit down and bide your time for at least an hour. Any vitally hit deer should die within that time and then you don't have to worry about jumping him. You can feel especially confident about that if you find heavy blood sign.

If you don't find much blood, the deer either could be bleeding internally, in which case he'll probably die quickly, or he's not bleeding much at all. The second choice could mean a hit in the stomach or intestines. If for any reason you think you've hit a deer in the paunch, leave him alone for 5 or 6 hours. He'll lie down within a short distance and will die eventually, but it will take time. You absolutely don't want to make him run because he can go miles and will leave virtually no trail. Just give him time, and then track him carefully.

TRAILING

As I've said, well-placed arrows don't kill by hemorrhage. Rather, they destroy major organs and animals die almost instantly. Marginal hits, on the other hand, do kill by hemorrhage, and an animal can travel some distance before it bleeds to death. That's where trailing knowledge comes in.

A few years back, I wrote an article and quoted an experienced hunter as saying he enjoyed trailing and considered it an important part of the hunt. An editor returned the article because, he said, it made the hunter sound like a barbarian who enjoyed wounding animals so he'd have the pleasure of trailing them.

The editor missed the point. Nobody in his right mind enjoys wounding animals, but no hunter can guarantee perfect shots every time. Sooner or later you could hit a deer in the liver, leg or paunch, and even though that animal will bleed to death, he'll probably go a long way before he drops. Even a heart or lung shot animal can cover 100 yards or more before it goes down and you might have to trail it. As a result, trailing plays a big part in bowhunting, and it must be perfected right along with spotting, stalking, or shooting. You might as well learn to enjoy it along with the rest of hunting.

Accepting that fact solves 90 percent of all trailing problems, because the will to succeed breeds the way. If, after hitting an animal, you just look around and find no blood and give up right there, chances are you're leaving animals you could recover. That's particularly possible on edge hits that seem nonlethal. The tendency is to say, "It just nicked him, so no sense in looking for that one. He'll heal right up."

It is true that many arrow-hit animals survive. In one region, rifle hunters were up in arms against bowhunting because they — the rifle hunters — had killed a couple elk with broadheads in them. They condemned bowhunting as a result, but I think that example commends bowhunting. In many cases, animals fully recover from marginal arrow wounds.

On the other hand, no bowhunter has the right to use that as an excuse not to search for an animal. Frequently you can't judge the nature of a hit from an animal's reaction or blood sign. One friend of mine shot at an elk and his arrow deflected off a branch and hit the elk in the hoof. Most hunters wouldn't consider searching for that animal. How in the world could a hoof hit kill an elk?

But my friend found a speck of blood, so he started trailing and kept at it for several hours until he could find no more sign. It seemed hopeless, but not one to give up, this fellow returned the next morning and searched systematically. And he found the elk dead. The arrow had cut an artery just behind the hoof and the animal had bled to death.

The lesson should be clear enough. Don't give up hope until all hope is gone. Armed with nothing other than that philosophy, you'll recover 90 percent of the game you ever hit, because if you have a strong enough desire to succeed, you'll find ways to do it.

Still, some pointers on the mechanics of trailing can help. My friend Larry Jones is an indefatigable game trailer. He won't give up, and through dedication and practice he's developed the skill to follow a trail that would baffle a bloodhound.

STAY ON THE TRAIL. One lesson Larry has taught me is to stick with the trail. That might seem obvious, but when a trail gets sparse, some of us get impatient and course out ahead like bird dogs, hoping to stumble onto the animal or luck onto obvious blood sign. Along this line, writers often advise that you anticipate where an animal will go and to search there. Often while hunting with Larry, I've heeded that advice and wandered around searching places where a wounded animal most likely would go. At the same time, Larry has patiently snooped around looking for the trail, and time after time he has picked up the trail again, heading in the opposite direction I'd been searching. Anymore I don't put much credence in the theories that wounded animals will head downhill, or they'll seek heavy cover or whatever. Predicting an animal's movement involves too many variables. Sleuth out his trail instead.

Obviously you're first looking for blood. On a lung or heart shot animal you won't have to look hard to find it, and you probably won't have to

In trailing an animal you may have to get down and crawl because that's the only way you'll spot tiny drops of blood or other sign. Larry Jones, shown here, has proved to me many times that you'll do best if you stick with the trail rather than coursing out to look for the animal.

look far for the animal. But in many cases mortally wounded animals will bleed internally, leaving a sparse trail. That's especially true if you're shooting downhill and your arrow hits high, or if it passes through the paunch on the way to the lungs. The stomach and intestines will seal up an arrow hole so little if any blood will escape externally, even if the deer is bleeding heavily.

Never assume that blood will be easy to see. It may be, but often you have to look closely. If you just walk along, crouched over, you'll miss all but the most obvious sign. Often I've done that and would swear up and down the bleeding had stopped. Then I'll get down on my hands and knees and really look close, and the trail will be obvious. My reaction is, "How could I miss that in the first place?"

If an animal circles, you could end up trailing it the wrong way, so inspect blood drops to see which way the deer is going. When an animal is moving, blood makes a big splotch when it hits the ground and sprays out in several tiny drops. The deer is heading toward the side with the little drops. If blood drops are round, the deer probably is standing still.

CRAWL. If you have to crawl to follow the trail, then humble yourself and crawl. Late one evening, I shot an elk and the animal covered a lot of ground in a hurry. Before long darkness set it, and I had to trail with a small emergency flashlight. In the dim beam I could scarcely see the ground, let alone blood, so I crawled and was amazed at how easily I could detect spots of blood the size of a pinhead. It was only because my face was right to the ground, close enough to see well.

Getting close to the ground like that not only gives a closeup view, but it gives you a better angle to spot some kinds of blood. Frequently blood running down an animal's leg or side won't drip onto the ground, but it will smear onto bushes and grass. Looking down from a standing position, you may never see blood on the undersides of grass or leaves, but from a low angle looking up, you'll quickly notice dark smears on vegetation. Larry and I have trailed animals this way when virtually no blood had dripped onto the ground.

TRAILING AT NIGHT. You often read that you shouldn't shoot a deer in late afternoon because you might not find him before dark. Certainly you're more likely to end up looking after dark if you shoot a buck late, but you could end up trailing in the dark no matter when you shoot a buck, so prepare yourself.

Actually trailing at night isn't hard. As I've said, you might be even more effective than during the day because you're forced to get down and look closer. You can see blood very well in the beam of a bright flashlight, but a gas lantern works even better. One hunter said he uses a lantern with a reflector on one side to keep the light out of his eyes, and he feels

Mike Cupell, shown here in the Arizona desert, often marks a blood trail with plastic tape to keep him on track.

he can trail more surely in the intense lantern light than in the natural light of day.

TRACKING. Most trailing involves looking for blood, but even a hard-hit deer could leave a skimpy blood trail, so learn to look for other signs, too. Here again, you may have to get down on your knees and look close to find them, but if you really fine-tune your perceptions, you'll notice all kinds of things you'd normally overlook. You'll see an overturned pebble, a broken twig, or a smear of mud on a rock. All of these could be signs of your animal's passing.

One time game warden Paul Mustain made a case by tracking a deer that didn't bleed. He had seen a man shoot from the back of a pickup, so Mustain pulled the truck over.

"What are you shooting at?" he said.

"Nothing," the man growled. "I just felt like shootin'."

Mustain went into the woods to look around. He found no blood, so he got on his knees to look across the ground. It was an overcast day with high humidity, and oak leaves on the ground looked shiny. But Mustain could see several dull-looking, dry leaves spaced 4 to 5 feet apart. He lined out on these, and they led him to a forked-horn buck. The buck had kicked up the leaves as it ran. Mustain made a case against the man who shot the deer.

As you trail a deer, inspect the tracks and impregnate your mind with their peculiar look. All animal tracks are distinct, and a wounded animal in particular may leave a clearly recognizable track. Larry and I tracked a Coues deer in Arizona. The deer wasn't leaving drag marks or other obvious indicators, but we got so tuned into the specific size and freshness of its track that we could recognize it at a glance, and even on hard ground we unwaveringly followed that deer.

Plastic marking tape can help in trailing an animal. If you mark the trail every few yards, you can look back to see the course. Then, if you simply can no longer follow the trail, you can circle ahead to look for the animal and then return to the trail easily, and taking a line on the trail can help you predict where the animal might go. Mike Cupell shot a deer that disappeared over a hill. Flagging as he went, Cupell followed the scant trail as far as possible, and when the trail played out, he sighted along the flag line.

"That buck is bedded right there," he said to himself, noting a small patch of cover in line with the flags. He circled to get the wind in his favor then sneaked toward the brush and found the buck within 10 yards of where he'd predicted.

Maybe trailing wounded animals doesn't seem like an exciting part of hunting, but it's more important than any other because, after the shot, it's the link between you and your trophy. If you recognize trailing as an integral part of bowhunting and perfect it along with other skills, you'll be the complete — and successful — bowhunter.

CHAPTER 10

OTHER METHODS

As you've probably gathered by now, I think spotting and stalking is the way to hunt mule deer — and all western deer for that matter. But, then, who's to say I'm right? A lot of hunters disagree with me, and some of them have hunting records that far better support their claims than mine do mine.

And it is true than an adaptable hunter can take advantage of various situations that would stymie the one-method hunter. You might take the buck of a lifetime if you can assess a situation and tailor your approach to unique conditions. As Harold Boyack said, "I just do whatever is needed."

MODIFIED STALKING

Actually Boyack's philosophy doesn't differ a whole lot from mine. He hunts primarily with his eyes, and he loves canyon country where he can see from one side into brush on the other so he can always spot bucks well before they see him. With a deer in view, he then can plan a stalk that will put him within bow range of the animal.

In contrast to my approach, however, he prefers not to stalk bedded deer. I suspect that's partly because he hunts a different kind of country. Boyack has taken most of his largest bucks in Utah and Colorado where serviceberries, oak brush, aspens and other cover is fairly heavy. In this kind of country, you can have a hard time just finding a buck once he's bedded. More of my hunting has taken place in open sagebrush country of the Great Basin where bucks will feed and bed right out in the open, a mile from any cover, so you have to go after them there, and that's possible only after they've lain down.

Boyack primarily tries to ambush a buck. Once he's spotted a feeding animal, he watches it long enough to anticipate its movements. Often he'll spot a buck feeding early in the morning toward the bottom of a canyon. He knows it will bed higher where it can see and catch the rising midday breeze, so Boyack anticipates the buck's route uphill and tries to ambush the deer at some point along the way.

"I like to let a buck come to me. That's a lot easier than going to him," Boyack said. "They don't seem as alert, and I can wait in just the right place so the buck must present a good shot. In some places it's hard to get a clean shot at a bedded buck, but when a buck is walking up to me, I can look around and find just the right place to get a good shot.

"As soon as I've spotted a moving buck and gauge where he's going, I hurry at first to get into position ahead of him, then I pick a spot and wait. I like to hunt a place used heavily by cattle, because cows make nice soft trails that help in stalking.

"A couple of different days in Colorado, I'd watched a buck go up through a cliff to his bedding area, so one morning I planted myself there and waited," Boyack related. "He walked up through that cliff and stopped 12 feet from me. That's my kind of hunting. I loved it."

AMBUSH

USING NATURAL MOVEMENTS. A fine line separates the stalking ambush and stand hunting, and at some point they must merge. Chuck Warner is another successful mule deer hunter who glasses and then stalks to ambush bucks, but he also turns to stand hunting when he has watched a buck long enough to figure out its regular movements.

In one instance, Warner heard some hunters discussing a big nontypical buck in southern Oregon, so he took several weekend scouting trips to the vicinity they'd mentioned, and he found a set of very large deer tracks mixed among smaller ones. During several different trips he studied tracks in the area and found they generally moved from a high, timbered basin around a rock bluff, through a saddle and down into a lush valley. Warner figured the deer fed in the valley at night and bedded above the bluff during the day.

He built a ground blind on the downwind side of the saddle several weeks before the season opened so deer in the area would get used to it. Opening weekend he waited there and saw several does and smaller bucks but not the big one he was after. But tracks told him a big buck still habitually used trails through the saddle, so he returned with confidence the following weekend, and late one afternoon he nailed the big buck he wanted as it walked through the saddle at close range. This nontypical mule deer scored 185 7/8.

Warner bases his strategy on the habitual nature of deer, and he has proven with his success that mule deer follow patterns closely enough to be hunted from a stand. He's found that mountain deer filter down ridges and canyons in the evenings to feed and water, and during early morning hours they climb back up to bed high. He has ambushed many bucks, using both tree stands and ground blinds, as they returned to their bedding areas in the mornings. He particularly seeks out remote areas where deer can carry on undisturbed so he can figure out their natural movements. In heavily hunted areas, he thinks you just have to be lucky to have someone run a good one by you.

USING OTHER HUNTERS. On the other hand, you may be able to put other hunters to work for you. I've tried stalking bucks on Labor Day weekend in popular areas and have just about given it up. With lots of hunters roaming around, you'll have a hard time finding an undisturbed buck to stalk, so you might have better success hunting from a stand.

Clark Unruh has ambushed several bucks, even in wide open desert country, by anticipating what other hunters might do. On opening day at Hart Mountain in eastern Oregon, hordes of hunters often ascend the mountain from below, and they push deer toward the top ahead of them. Unruh found a slot where several deer trails converged between a rock slide on one side and tangled aspen on the other.

"The terrain there just about forced any deer coming up the mountain to go through that one spot, and most of the shots I got there were very close."

Unruh said he prefers glassing and stalking to stand hunting because it's a lot more fun, but he doesn't deny the efficiency of a stand. He killed deer from that one stand three out of four years.

TREE STANDS

When John Lamicq, a Colorado outfitter, first started guiding bowhunters, he found that many eastern hunters who'd hunted primarily from tree stands couldn't stalk well enough to take deer at ground level, so he started building tree stands. In Lamicq's sage and aspen country of northwest Colorado, mule deer habitually use the same routes to and from feeding areas day after day, year after year, so once he learned these routes, Lamicq knew right where to put his stands. He has used some of the same tree stands since 1965. Each year he now takes 50 to 60 bowhunters, and they have about a 50 percent success rate, much higher than Colorado's overall average for bowhunters. Obviously his tree stand tactics work well.

Dave Snyder is another bowhunter who believes in tree stands, particularly for big bucks. Snyder has killed several huge bucks, including a Utah mule deer that ranks No. 3 in Pope and Young, as well the world-record non-typical Coues whitetail from Arizona. (Snyder also killed the world-record Rocky Mountain elk.) Snyder thinks big mule deer are habitual, possibly as much so as whitetails, and that's why stands work well. He also likes hunting from a tree stand because it gets his scent up off the ground and deer don't see him up there. He can hunt an area day after day without spooking deer, and he can put himself in the movement range of the animal to get a good shot.

"You can pattern big mulies," Snyder said. "You might not find them using the same trails day after day, as you might on whitetails, but you'll find them within 80 to 100 to 150 yards of the same trail. Big bucks hang out in a small area and don't move around much. That's why you don't see many of them. If you put your stand in the right spot your big buck will eventually come by, although you may have to move your stand to get it just right."

Snyder scouts as much as possible to locate a trophy class buck, but he does it at a distance to avoid bothering the deer he wants to hunt.

"If someone hired me as a hit man to knock off my neighbor, I'd watch that neighbor's every move to plan an infallible ambush, but I sure wouldn't let him know I was doing it," Snyder said. "It's the same way with hunting a big buck. You want to know exactly what he's doing without disturbing him. Once a big buck is spooked, he's much harder to find after that. I saw the three largest bucks I've taken many times before I shot them. I saw that Coues whitetail nine consecutive days, and the mule deer in Utah I saw twice."

Snyder also scouts for sign to pattern a buck. He said: "Every buck has to eat, drink, crap. He leaves tracks. You can figure him out from all that, and you want to catch him leaving or going to his bed.

"I like to hunt bedding areas because that's where big bucks will hang out after they've been disturbed. They'll quit feeding in the open and will start hanging out all day in denser bedding cover.

"That's one thing many hunters overlook. They scout before the season and put up their tree stands right where they last saw a good buck. On opening day, hunters might kick that buck out of there, and you've got to anticipate where he'll go and where he'll hang out when the pressure is on."

WATERHOLE STANDS

In dry country, water serves as the focal point for all deer activity, and waterhole stands can be deadly. My friend Mike Cupell hunts waterholes effectively in Arizona, particularly in the Sonoran desert south of Phoenix. He emphasizes that the weather must be hot and dry for good hunting. After a rain, deer have little reason to come to standing water.

In areas with several large stock tanks, Cupell said the biggest animals may sneak into small, hidden seeps or trickle tanks. He thinks a tree stand assures the best chance for a shot, but he likes ground blinds better because they put him at eye level with game. One time a doe stuck her head right into his blind, and he figures that's the kind of experience that

Waterhole stands can produce big bucks if conditions are right. Russ Suminski shot this 10 by 13, 35-inch buck as it came to a spring in dry, desert country.

makes hunting fun.

To be comfortable in a ground blind, he packs a small cooler in which he carries water and snacks, and he uses it as a stool in his blind. He has made a camouflage cover for it and has glued carpet to the bottom to prevent grating noises on the ground.

WATERHOLE SUCCESS. Nevada bowhunter Russell Suminski has put stands to work for him. As he points out, in the open country of Nevada, you must find a place where deer concentrate to use a stand effectively, and primarily that means water during a dry year.

Suminski's wife is a wildlife biologist, and one dry summer as she worked in the field she discovered a spring where deer had been coming to drink. The weekend before opening day, she and Russ returned to build a blind, 25 yards from a trail that led to the spring.

Opening morning, Russ didn't have to wait long for action. Right at daylight four 4-point bucks walked down the trail in front of him and as two of them stopped to feed, the other two walked directly to the spring for water. As they drank, Russ shot and missed.

That was his only action for the morning, so he went back to camp to tell his wife about the experience, and then he returned to his stand late that afternoon. Long shadows had just engulfed the canyon when he again saw a deer coming. A large 4-point came within 10 feet but the buck saw Russ drawing his bow and pranced away. As Russ watched this deer, trying to figure out how to get a shot, a larger buck appeared from the brush and headed toward the spring. Suminski drew and waited as the buck walked by, and then released an arrow as the deer moved into the open at the spring. His arrow hit home. He'd bagged a mule deer with 10 points on one side, 13 on the other, and a 35-inch maximum spread, not a bad buck for starters.

CHAPTER 11

TACKLE AND GEAR

Tackle and other kinds of gear in themselves might not guarantee anything, but they do contribute to a hunt. If nothing else the right gear gives you confidence, and it also saves you time and guarantees comfort. I don't offer the following as any kind of set formula because you might have plenty of better ideas, and it seems to me no two hunters ever agree on choosing tackle and gear.

Still, hunters commonly ask what kind of tackle I use and what kind of clothing is best for deer hunting, so for whatever they're worth, I'll offer a few opinions. In no way is this a complete discussion of tackle and other gear. That would take a whole book in itself. These are just some thoughts on equipment that can affect the outcome of a deer hunt.

ARCHERY TACKLE

BOWS. In choosing a bow, killing power really isn't the issue. Most states have laws that require deer hunters to use bows heavier than 40 pounds draw weight, and in my opinion, any legal bow has more than enough power to kill a deer within reasonable range. For that reason, women and youngsters who can pull no more than 40 pounds can hunt deer with confidence.

The qualifying phrase there is "reasonable range." The effective range of a bow is related more closely to trajectory than penetration. Even light bows will penetrate well enough, but their reasonable range is somewhat limited and a person shooting a light bow must recognize the limitations and go for close shots.

And that's why lighter bows can be a handicap. As I've said earlier, open-country hunting doesn't guarantee you the close shots you'd expect in treestand hunting for whitetails. In many situations you indeed can get 20-yard shots, but to give yourself the best overall odds, you should be able to shoot accurately out to at least 50 yards. You can do that most consistently with a relatively fast-shooting bow, something that shoots an arrow in the 200 feet-per-second class, give or take a few feet. Most compound bows in the 60-pound class will shoot a 600-grain arrow that fast, and many recurves will, too, so just about any bow in this category serves well for western deer. Recently I've been shooting a Hoyt-Easton Prohunter set at 55 pounds. This bow shoots a 580-grain 2117 at 194 feet per second, and my older Jennings T-Star shot comparably. I feel confident out to 50 yards with these bows.

Recurve bows are inherently as accurate as compound bows, but most hunters can shoot a compound better because they can hold it at full draw more comfortably and aim longer. If you stalk well, you'll have plenty of time to draw and aim, and this deliberate kind of shooting fits perfectly into the compound-bow mold. At times you'll get caught off guard, or you'll draw and then must wait for a buck to turn, and holding a compound bow under these circumstances gives you a real edge. With a recurve most of us would have to let up if we couldn't release an arrow right away. The ability to hold on target for several seconds to a half-minute or more can make all the difference in some cases.

We could get into a book-length discussion on compounds vs. recurves vs. longbows, and we'd get nowhere because most hunters' preferences are a matter of philosophy. My intent is only to describe what I consider the most effective gear. If you have time to practice hours a day and can develop a smooth, instinctive shooting style, they you'll probably do as well with a stick bow as with a compound. Some of the most successful hunters in North America use nothing but recurves and long bows. I respect their ability and admire their dedication to tradition, but I think the average bowhunter will become a far more competent game shot using a compound bow.

SIGHTS. In recent years, bow sights have become commonplace. I more or less take them for granted, but many hunters still ask me whether I think they'd gain anything by using sights as opposed to shooting bare bow. In my opinion, you'll shoot better with sights.

A few years back I went on a "traditional" kick and took the sights off my bow and decided to be a real bowhunter, just like Fred Bear, shooting a recurve bow instinctively. Frankly, it felt good. I was no longer one of those modern junkies, shooting all that technological garbage. I practiced long and hard to develop my shooting ability and quite honestly could shoot as well without sights as with.

Then came bow season, and the hunting was fantastic. In 10 days of deer hunting I missed 9 shots ranging from 15 to 40 yards. After the last miss I was about ready to give up bowhunting altogether. But instead I decided to swallow my pride and try the sights one more time. With the same bow, a 60-pound Kittredge recurve, only now equipped with sights, my next three shots brought down two animals, an elk and a deer. My confidence was restored.

The sights didn't make me a better shot necessarily, but they did make me a better game shot. Why? Because they gave me a positive aiming reference point. Shooting bare bow, you must either aim by judging the gap between your broadhead and the spot you want to hit, or you mentally visualize the trajectory of your arrow to the animal. To do that you must maintain extreme concentration as you shoot at an animal. Without sights my concentration just went to pot, but sights forced me to pick a certain pin and to place that pin on the animal's chest, and this mechanical process forced me to concentrate long enough to make a good shot.

I've talked to many other bowhunters about this subject, and most relate similar opinions. The sights help them to pick a spot and aim during the heat of action, and as a result they shoot better on game. Unless you can practice an hour or more a day to develop truly exceptional barebow skills, I think you'll do better on open-country deer shooting with sights.

My sight has four pins set at 25, 35, 45 and 55 yards. Some hunters have six or eight pins, but I find that many confusing. Why 25, 35 and so forth, rather than 20, 30, 40? Who knows? Just to be different, I guess.

RANGEFINDERS. In open-country hunting, especially when you're crouched low in the brush looking at just a deer's antler tips, judging range can be tough. A rangefinder can help. Here again these fall under the heading — in some hunter's minds — of modern technological garbage, because they seemingly take all of the hunt out of hunting. Believe me, a rangefinder guarantees you nothing. The fact is, you must have time to use one of these gadgets, so a deer must be unaware of your presence, and he must be in the open where you can get a clear view of him. To satisfy those requirements, you have to make one heckuva good stalk. In some cases, trying to use a rangefinder will actually cost you a shot when a buck catches you fiddling around with the 'finder.

BROADHEADS. Any modern broadhead will do the job on deer. I've shot several animals with Razorbak 4 broadheads, which have a pointed, pencil-like tip and razorblade inserts, and these have performed well. If you won't take time to sharpen broadheads, I'd suggest you use these or other comparable modular broadheads with presharpened blades.

On the other hand, I have far more faith in broadheads with a cutting tip. One time I shot a pig from a diagonal angle, back to front, and my arrow, tipped with a modular broadhead, literally glanced off the side of that animal. Rather than penetrating, the round, pencil-like tip of the broadhead slid along the hide and deflected straight up. A broadhead with a sharp leading edge would have sliced through the hide.

Deer have much thinner hides than pigs, so that analogy might not hold

When you're crouched low in the sage, judging range can be tough. A good rangefinder can help considerably although it's by no means foolproof. You need a clear view of the deer, and the deer must be unaware of your presence, which calls for super stalking ability.

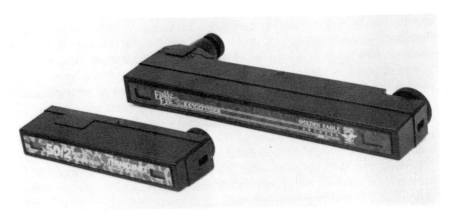

The Ranging 50/2 and the Golden Eagle 3X Eagle Eye rangefinders are two good models for bowhunters. Don't think these will solve all your problems, though, because you still have to stalk well to make them work.

up, but still it offers a warning. If you hit a deer at a strong diagonal angle, a pencil point could deflect off a rib, whereas a broadhead with a cutting edge right to the tip would cut through the rib.

Penetration could be an issue, too. Any good broadhead will shoot through a deer broadside, but again, if you're shooting diagonally, your arrow will have to cut full length of the body to reach lungs or heart. Modular broadheads more or less push through tissue while sharpened heads cut through. To judge the difference, clamp a modular broadhead with a pencil-type point, and a head sharpened right to the tip, in a vice and then pull a piece of leather down over each one until the head cuts through the leather. You'll find that the sharpened head requires much less force to slice through. Zwickey Black Diamond heads are hard to beat, and Bear's new stainless steel Razorheads are good, too.

OTHER TACKLE. Should arrows be fletched with feathers or vanes? Both can be made to shoot equally well, so in my mind that's not the question. For two reasons I strongly favor plastic vanes. One, they're more durable. Rain doesn't affect them, and you won't tear them up dragging them through brush. Two, they're quieter. Feathers scratching through sagebrush during a stalk drives me nuts. And spooks deer. From a noise point of view, comparing feathers to vanes is like comparing denim to wool.

Your tackle must be tight to eliminate all rattling. Modern plastic bow quivers with a quick release bracket are handy, but they can rattle, and they pop loudly when you shoot. I far prefer other styles. One super quiver is the Sagittarius Pegasus, which bolts under the limb bolts on your bow. It simply can't rattle unless your bow limbs are loose enough to fall off. The Bear bow quiver, which is made of steel just as it has been since time began, also is a solid, quiet quiver.

When you draw at close range, a deer could hear your arrow hissing across metal, so use a rubber or teflon-coated rest, and pad the sides of the bow window so your arrow won't clatter if you accidentally pull it off the rest. Also, if your bow has a slide on the cable guard, try drawing when this is wet to make sure it's quiet. On my bow this slide squeaks when it's wet. To reduce cable wear, I practice with the slide on the cables, but I take it off for hunting. The bow shoots just as well without it.

CLOTHES

Quietness is the No. 1 criterion for choosing clothes. Camouflage clothing has become a fetish in recent years, but as I've said before, the overall hue means a lot more than a camo pattern. Any olive drab or gray clothing will work, and if it comes down to choosing between quiet, solid-color clothing, or noisy camouflage, I'll take the quiet stuff any day.

During August seasons, you'll face hot weather so you have to have lightweight clothes. That pretty much means cotton, or a cotton blend. It seems to me cotton clothes have a universal problem — they're noisy. They rustle and swish, particularly when they're wet. Some fabrics are worse than others, though, so shop around and pick the softest material you can find, and then wash it and pound it until it's soft and quiet. One company makes clothes like sweat-suit material, and these are super quiet.

In cooler weather, I just get rid of cotton altogether and go to wool or knit clothes. Writers have said "wear wool" so many times I hate to say it just because it brands me as another typical writer. Still, the truth remains unchanged. Wool is great. So what the heck? Wear wool. You can get very lightweight wool that's scarcely warmer than cotton, so you can wear it under most any conditions. In recent years I've gone to knickers for much of my hunting. Some macho guys laugh because I look like a pixie, but let them laugh. Pants cuffs serve only one function — they give sagebrush something to tear up. Wearing knickers, I save a lot of money because I don't have to buy new pants every season, and besides they're a lot quieter than pants. The long socks fit my legs like skin, which allows absolutely silent sneaking.

Knit clothes perform well, too. Some synthetic knits aren't quite as durable as woven wool, but they're superior in that they dry a lot faster, which can be great when you're regularly getting hit with rain. Bob Fratzke's knit acrylic hunting clothes are warm, soft and quiet. I've fallen in love with his line of clothing and wear it frequently during cool weather.

Probably one of the toughest clothing assignments for early-season deer hunting is reconciling hot and cold weather. You can expect heat, but just as surely you'd better plan for cold. Include wool clothes and long underwear, as well as raingear, a warm hat, gloves and so forth on every hunt.

In terms of footwear, I like the new hiking shoes made like running shoes. They have a soft, cushioned sole for comfort, and they're lightweight so you don't feel like you have bricks tied to your feet. For wet weather hunting, the rubber-bottom, leather-top boots, like Bean's Maine Hiking Shoe, are hard to beat. Many modern lightweight hiking shoes contain a Gore-Tex sleeve, which supposedly makes them waterproof and some hunters swear by these, but I've had a half-dozen pairs and have yet to find one that's waterproof. Even at that they're better for all-around hunting than heavy leather boots. Anymore, the only place I can see for heavy leather boots is when you're carrying a heavy load. They give good ankle support and foot protection.

PREPARE FOR EVERY SITUATION

One time some hunters told me about all the deer they saw way up on a mountain, but they had only three days and just didn't have time to go up there after them because they'd spend all their time hiking up and down if they tried to hunt that far from a road. So they settled for the more accessible stuff. And poor hunting.

I said something under "Planning" that's worth bringing up again here: If any one aspect of hunting deserves credit for my success, it's location. WHERE I hunt has a lot more to do with quality than HOW I hunt. The "where" begins with planning and research, but in the end it comes down to equipment. Deer won't come to you; you have to go to them, so

Quietness is the No. 1 criterion for choosing clothes. In cool weather, knit acrylic clothing like that made by Bob Fratzke's Winona Mills can't be beat. Here Larry Jones wears knit pants, sweater, hat and gloves — clothes that are warm and quiet.

prepare ahead of time to do just that. You won't be disappointed.

DAY PACK. Good hunting starts with the gear you carry each day. As we've discussed you'll spot the most deer early and late in the day, and to

Good hunting starts with good location, and you'll rarely find the best concentration of bucks near roads. Go prepared to hunt backcountry where deer will congregate after the shooting starts. Larry Jones has loaded up his backpack for several days of wilderness hunting.

hunt these times you have to leave camp before daylight in the morning, and you'll probably return after dark at night. Not only will you do a lot of walking in the dark, but you could get lost on occasion. You have to prepare for that. I always carry a small fanny pack with the essential items for edge-of-night hunting. A lot of hunters consider this survival gear — and it definitely could save your life — but to my way of thinking it's hunting-efficiency gear.

A flashlight tops the list, because you'll often need it to find your way in the dark.

If you're worried about getting lost and freezing to death, you'll obviously avoid hunting late or far from camp, so other items are important. Two are map and compass. In some country, walking in a straight line after dark is nearly impossible. With a compass you can travel a known direction or maintain a straight line of travel to hit a trail or road, and with a map you can figure out your position, which you probably can't do without it.

A good fire starter ranks high on the list, too. You may visualize western hunting as high and dry, but don't kid yourself. Even in the desert you'll get soaked by endless rains, and when hunting above timberline in the high mountains you can predict right now that drenching thunderstorms and snow will be part of your hunt. When you get wet, a fire could be the one thing that will save your life. Carry a butane lighter, waterproof matches, and a fire starter such as pitchwood or Heat Tabs to assure that you can build a fire. In really wet weather, I also carry shelter, such as a lightweight square of plastic, with which to build an emergency lean-to.

WATER. In many high mountain ranges, springs and creeks are abundant and you'll find more than enough water. In desert and prairie country, that's rarely the case. Water will be scarce, and even if it's not, it well could be polluted by livestock. I've tried hunting all day without water in hot weather, but it doesn't work. You get too dehydrated to hunt well. For that reason, you have to carry water. A bota bag — some people call it a wineskin — works well because you can squeeze out the air after you drink to prevent sloshing. For all day hunting, carry at least a quart of water.

Bucks won't come to you so you have to go to them. That could mean a long haul into remote country, so prepare to stay out for a few nights. Larry Jones and I set up this comfortable backpack camp in Utah, and we had great hunting withing sight of camp.

You also can carry a piece of surgical tubing about 3 feet long and a cup. You can poke one end of the tube into even the tiniest seeping spring and siphon pure water into the cup, and you can use the tubing to refill your bota bag or canteen.

CAMPING GEAR. On any hunt you're wise to plan several modes of camping. For mobile hunting, you might hunt from a road and sleep in the canopy of your pickup wherever you end up at night. Or you might prefer a more permanent tent or travel trailer. One way or the other, a good base camp where you can dry clothes, get a good meal, and warm up through and through can turn a fizzling hunt into a memorable adventure. Without a good camp, any slightly nasty weather can send you home in a whining panic.

A good base camp, however, doesn't allow much flexibility. As I've said, the animals won't come to you so you have to go to them, and that means mobility. My standard gear on every hunt includes a backpack and some lightweight groceries and gear. You may plan to camp at your car, but when you arrive on the scene you might discover an enticing alpine bowl high on a distant ridge. If it's a 5-hour hike from the road, you hardly can hunt from your car each day, but with a backpack and a few days' rations, you can move your base of operations right up there and hunt comfortably with very little walking each day.

I often carry that a step further and prepare to bivouac, which means I can stuff a light sleeping bag and a couple of days' supplies into my daypack and head out crosscountry, sleeping wherever I end up that night. As mentioned earlier, Cliff Dewell often does this so he can be glassing a remote spot right at daylight. When I want to look over a new canyon or ridge and don't want to pack a heavy load for several days, I'll bivouac out a night or two just for a quick investigation. If things look good, I'll load up the big backpack and return prepared to stay for several days.

QUICK HUNT

That all reminds me of a trip to the desert. It was one of those makeshift two-day trips we all squeeze in once in awhile when we know we really shouldn't go, but do it anyway just because we can't help ourselves. The press of business had kept me from really thinking ahead, so when the time came, I just chucked everything in the truck in a half-hour and drove.

For a trip like this I don't take any elaborate camp, but I do make sure I have my backpack and other necessary gear to cover every situation. I'd done enough research to know the quality of deer here, but I didn't know the country, and in my hurry to leave, I'd forgotten my maps. With the right gear, at least, I was prepared to do whatever was necessary to find deer quickly.

By the time I arrived at 7:30 p.m., night was coming on. One look at the country proved I'd have to do some hiking — about 2 miles straight up

— to get to the deer, and doing that before daylight the next morning would be tough, particularly since I didn't even know where to go. So I threw together some bivouac gear and started hiking.

Right at dark I found a deer bed under a rock — the only flat spot on that part of the mountain — and sacked out. Wind roaring through nearby limber pines woke me up well before daylight so I was ready to go plenty early, and by the first glow of daylight I was sitting on top of a ridge, overlooking a beautiful basin where aspen trees at the lower end gave way to open sage higher up.

I leaned against a boulder to glass the basin, and instantly a buck walked into view. Just uphill another buck was feeding in some scrub aspen. And farther away stood two more, and eventually I'd spotted seven bucks there.

I slipped into the aspen grove below the bucks and followed along below them. As they fed out of sight over the top of a hill, I sprinted toward them to narrow the distance quickly and then slipped off my boots and closed in.

At the top of the hill, the bucks had fed around a patch of scrubby aspen out of sight, so on hands and knees I crawled to the edge of the trees and sat down to rest. Then, just beyond the aspens, 20 yards away, I could hear the deer rustling leaves and chewing.

"Yipes," I thought. "They're right there. Get ready!"

Time was short on this hunt, but because I'd taken gear to cover any situation, I got into good deer country quickly. Taking this buck at first seemed like a miracle, but with some thought I realized it had happened just the way I'd planned it.

Peeking over, I could see the antlers of three small bucks. With an arrow nocked, I waited. Just uphill one of the bigger bucks, a 2-point, walked into view. Earlier I'd planned to hold out for a nice 4-point in the bunch, but he was nowhere in sight and here was a buck in the hand, as they say. With the wind whipping around, the deer could smell me any time, and I had only two days. Maybe I'd better not be too picky. I estimated the range at 40 yards — I had to shoot over several of the smaller bucks — and threaded an arrow through the buck's chest. He went only 50 yards and piled up.

I boned out the meat and loaded the entire deer, along with my camping gear, onto the packframe and headed down. It took all day to reach the truck and I was pretty well shot.

As I soaked my aching feet in the creek and stared at the buck tied to the backpack, my one emotion was satisfaction. This seemed like nothing short of a miracle, to kill a buck on the first day in a spot I'd never seen before. But then it shouldn't have been any big surprise. I'd done my homework to find this spot, and I'd come prepared to hunt it. Actually, the whole thing turned out just as I'd planned it.

CHAPTER 12

MEAT CARE AND PHYSICAL CONDITION

Meat care seems to be one aspect of early-season, off-road hunting that scares some hunters. They fear their deer will spoil before they can get it to cold storage. Certainly hot weather gives less leeway than cold, but you can still kill a deer in August heat and save it with no problem.

COOL HIM QUICK. Bone sour presents the most immediate, if not the major, meat-care problem. Meat spoils in two ways — from the inside out and the outside in. Bone sour is internal spoilage and it results from slow cooling. Meat scientists explain it this way. When an animal dies its organs stop, but its muscle cells continue to work, and in the process they create heat. In a live animal, circulating blood carries away excess heat to keep the animal's temperature at about 101 degrees, but in a dead animal the cooling system doesn't work and body temperatures can rise even higher than normal.

Bacteria within the meat grow best in temperatures from 60 to 100 degrees. If cooling is slow, bacteria will run wild and quickly sour the meat, but if you eliminate all body heat within 24 hours, bacterial growth stops and bone sour isn't a concern. Souring is a function of temperature, not location, but it occurs most frequently in the hips and shoulders of animals because these places cool most slowly. Obviously, then, you want to cool your deer quickly to prevent bone sour.

The first step is gutting, of course. An animal should be field-dressed as soon as it's down. Then comes the question of skinning. Deer will cool with the hide on, and if temperatures at night are dropping into the 30s or low 40s, you can just gut an animal and spread it open over rocks or logs to ensure good air circulation, and it will cool well overnight. Professor Ray Field, who has studied meat care extensively at the University of Wyoming, strongly advocates leaving the hide on animals in cool weather because hide keeps the meat clean and prevents drying. Studies have shown that hide does not affect taste.

In hot weather, when temperatures remain above 50 degrees at night, you'd better skin that animal immediately to cool it fast. Field's studies show that the thick part of a skinned deer leg drops to air temperature — in a cooler at 38 degrees — in 10 hours, but a hide-on leg requires 14 hours, so there's no question that skinning speeds up the cooling process.

You'll face two additional problems — dirt and flies — when you skin an animal in the field, however, so you should always carry game bags during warm weather. As soon as you've skinned your deer, slip it into a bag and hang it in the shade to cool. Normally I carry two tight-woven cheesecloth bags. For easy handling I cut the deer in half and slip the front half into one bag, the back into the other.

PACKING MEAT. One time a hunter told me he'd never return to a certain mountain because he and his friends killed a big buck 5 miles from the road there, and the country was so rough they nearly killed themselves dragging that buck down to the car.

Just THINKING about dragging a deer hurts my back. It's crazy. Maybe in some parts of the country where you can hunt next to a road the idea seems feasible, but in the West you can easily find yourself several miles from the road, and when that's the case packing is the only choice. That's another reason I always have a packframe handy. I'd rather pack a buck 10 miles than drag one 2.

You can cut a small buck in half and slip the hams inside the rib cage and tie it all to your packframe. The whole thing will weigh 60 to 70 pounds. On a bigger buck, you might prefer to make two trips. Generally on a big buck, I pack the back half in one whole piece. You can bone out the hams, but the leg bones don't weigh much and leaving them in makes the meat easier to handle.

I suggest boning out the front half. First cut off the front legs right at the shoulder and bone them out, and then fillet meat off the rib cage, neck and backbone in one big chunk. When you've done this you'll end up with a pile of pure meat that you can pack in one load. If you're really stout, you probably can pack an entire large buck in one load after boning it. With a big buck, you'll end up with 80 to 100 pounds.

HANGING THE MEAT. How long can you keep meat in camp? If you've cooled the meat well, bone sour shouldn't be a problem, but in warm weather bacteria will grow on the outside and meat will spoil from the outside in.

No exact guidelines say how long you can hang a deer in camp, because too many variables enter the picture. Some animals inherently contain more bacteria than others. An animal that has been run or frightened before it dies will deteriorate faster than one that was calm. A carcass with extensive, contaminating wounds will spoil more rapidly than a clean carcass. Meat will spoil faster in humid weather than in dry.

Still, some rough guidelines can be helpful. Commercial meat plants generally age beef for two weeks at 35 degrees, and they also quick-age meat for three days at 65 degrees. These figures don't apply directly to game meat because of the variables mentioned above, but they offer an idea of the outer limits. Commercial meat cutters go by the axiom, "Life begins at 40." If you can cool meat below 40 degrees — that's internal meat temperature, not air temperature — you can hang a deer in camp safely for a couple of weeks. With any increase in temperature, time decreases. At 65 degrees, you'd better get your deer into cold storage

I'd rather pack a deer 10 miles than to drag one for two. By boning, you can reduce even a big buck to a load weighing less than 100 pounds, and most hunters can handle that fairly well. You can also take shortcuts. I'd hate to try DRAGGING a buck over this cliff.

within three days or you could lose it.

If nights are cool and days are hot, you can still keep a deer fairly cool. To keep one buck in camp, I hung the skinned and quartered carcass to cool each night as air temperature dropped to 45 degrees. First thing each morning I stacked the meat on a tarp and wrapped it with sleeping bags. At the end of each day, after 12 hours in sleeping bags, internal meat temperature never rose above 48 degrees, and after seven days in camp, even though daytime temperatures were hitting 65, that meat was still as pink and sweet smelling as it was on the first day.

You can use the same method to transport meat home in your car. If you stack meat in the back of a pickup, put down a foam pad or other insulation under your deer. The exhaust system will heat the pickup bed and will spoil the meat.

Over the years I've hung deer in camp as long as a week, even in August, and have never lost any meat. With common sense and some precautions you can hunt early western seasons, confident you'll end up with great eating venison.

PHYSICAL CONDITION

You can make mule deer hunting as easy or tough as you want. As I've said you can spot deer right from your vehicle in many cases, and that way you don't have to waste any energy until you've actually spotted a deer.

Still, I don't think that's the way to hunt. In my opinion, the quality of hunting is related directly to the distance you hunt from the nearest road. The farther back you get, the more and bigger bucks will be. That's not always true, but it's true often enough that I'm willing to expend a lot of energy to reach some terrible spots.

I can't give any concrete figures on the distance you have to hike to find great hunting. Although I might sit for 3 or 4 hours in one spot, looking for deer, I'll probably hike several miles before daylight to get there, and I might move several times during the day to new spotting positions. Overall I'd say you can plan to hike from 5 to 8 miles a day in hunting mule deer.

Maybe more significant than distance is topography. Some mule deer country is fairly flat, but more commonly it's steep with 1,000 to 2,000 vertical feet separating the creek bottoms from the tops of the ridges. And much of it is high. You could be hunting anywhere from 6,000 feet elevation in the Great Basin deserts, to 12,000 feet in the mountains of Colorado. When you combine the distances, steepness and elevations of mule deer country, you have a good recipe for fatigue.

That's where physical condition comes in. Some hunters rely strictly on natural ability and youth to get them through, but most of us have to work hard to get in shape, and that means endurance, or aerobic, training. Running, walking, bicycle riding, cross country skiing — exercises you can sustain at a high level for a long period of time — fit into this category. These will prepare you best for hunting because they build a strong heart, lungs and legs, and that's what you need for mountain hunting.

If you've done no training, you should have a heart checkup before you start. Dr. Kenneth Cooper in his many books on aerobic training, says anyone with a family history of heart disease, regardless of age; and anyone over 35, should have a stress electrocardiogram (ECG) before starting a training program. A stress test will reveal abnormalities in the heart that won't show up on a resting ECG.

To be of value, aerobic workouts must meet at least two criteria: They must be sustained for a minimum of 20 minutes at your training heart rate (which is explained below), and they must be done at least three to five times a week.

Most physiologists recommend you begin aerobic training by walking. Walk for 10 minutes at a stiff pace, and increase that 2 to 3 minutes per week until you're up to 30 to 40 minutes a day. As you do this, keep your pulse rate at the recommended training rate. Use this formula to determine your training pulse rate:

220 - age = maximum heart rate X .70 (poor shape) = training rate
   X .80 (average shape)
   X .85 (excellent shape)

Here's an example. If you're 40 years old, you subtract your age from 220, which gives you a maximum heart rate of 180. Now, if you're in poor shape, you multiply 180 times .70, which gives you a training heart rate of 126 beats per minute. If you've been working out and consider yourself in good shape, then you multiply 180 times .80, which gives you a training rate of 144 beats per minute. To measure your pulse during a workout, exercise long enough to get your heart beating well, and then stop, count your pulse for 6 seconds and multiply by 10. If it comes out higher than the recommended training rate, slow down, and if it's lower, increase the intensity of your workout.

If you're in poor shape, you might find you can bring your heart rate up to the recommended level simply by walking. From that starting point, increase the amount of time you work out, and gradually increase your training heart rate. To do that, after your fitness level improves, you must increase your pace. After two months you may have to jog or run to attain the same heart rate you got by slow walking at first. That's good because it means you're getting in shape. It doesn't matter what kind of exercise you do as long as you maintain your training heart rate for at least 20 minutes or longer. The best aerobic exercises — walking, hiking, jogging, swimming, bicycling, rope skipping, calisthenics — utilize large muscles.

No one can say just how good your condition must be for sustained mountain hunting, because you can't directly correlate the energy required to do exercises with the energy demands of day-to-day hunting. However, I can make a subjective judgment based on my own experience. I generally run to keep in shape so that's my basis for comparison. During years when I've been running 2 to 3 miles a day, at least four days a week, I've been in adequate shape to handle a fairly tough hunt. Generally, I figure if I can go out and run 5 miles at will without straining, I can handle most hunting conditions.

That deserves some qualification, though. Running and most other aerobic exercises build strong heart and lungs, and they increase muscular endurance, but they don't necessarily develop strength or flexibility. If you plan to backpack or carry heavy loads, you should train specifically for that. A month or so before a hunt, put on your backpack loaded with 50 pounds (or as much as you can carry comfortably) and hike some hills or climb stairs for an hour each day, two or three days a week. This will save you from sore thighs and aching knees the first few days of a hunt, and it will strengthen your legs for the added strain of hiking up, down, and sidehill.

Weight training with barbells or on machines like the Universal Gym can build strength for hiking, too. Most towns these days have gyms with the right equipment and a qualified instructor. Working out there for two or three months before your hunt can be very beneficial. Don't substitute weight training for aerobic training, however. Weights will strengthen your muscles, but they don't do much for your heart and lungs, which are the organs that really count in long-distance hiking.

For more information on aerobic training, and for specific training programs to monitor your progress, I recommend any of Dr. Kenneth Cooper's aerobics books: *AEROBICS, THE NEW AEROBICS, THE AEROBICS WAY*, and *AEROBICS PROGRAM FOR TOTAL WELL BEING* (published in hardcover by M. Evans and Company, Inc., New York). I also recommend *FIT OR FAT?* by Covert Bailey (Houghton Mifflin Company, Boston).

CHAPTER 13

THE WAY IT IS

One morning Glenn Helgeland, a well-known writer from Wisconsin, and I sat on a hillside overlooking miles of rolling hills in northeastern Utah. The hills had an undercoating of purple sage with broken up clumps of serviceberry, mountain mahogany and aspen trees. The scene contained the perfect ingredients for mule deer.

As we watched some deer and waited for them to bed down before we planned a stalk, we had time to talk, and Glenn described some of his reactions to this thing we call western hunting.

"Back east 95 percent of our hunting is done from tree stands in the evening so this getting out early in the morning and watching for deer a long ways away is a new thing to me," Glenn said.

"Back there the brush is much denser. It's all timber hunting. The farthest I've ever shot a deer was 125 yards — that's with a rifle — and the closest was 18 inches. Out here you've got all these wide-open spaces and you can see deer miles away. Your shots potentially could be much longer.

"Back east, you're hunting as soon as you walk out the door or out of camp. Here it's a tremendous adjustment to realize that deer live in pockets, and that you have to find them before you can hunt them. You start looking at first light in the morning, and you can hunt all day and cover a lot of miles. Back east you could hunt all day in 200 acres, but out here you could hike 4 or 5 miles and you're just getting started."

THE REAL PICTURE

That conversation made me realize I take a lot of things in western hunting for granted. What we were doing had become second nature for me, but for Glenn it contained elements he'd never before experienced — and surprises he couldn't dream existed.

Some writers make hunting sound like nothing but smiles and gut piles. Those are part of it and I've enjoyed my share of each, but they don't tell the whole story, particularly of western hunting. I think it's unfair to build a perfect picture of any undertaking because it builds false expectations. If you've never participated, you think it's going to be one way and when it turns out another, you're disappointed. Mule deer hunting indeed can generate more joy than any form of hunting, but it can generate more grief, too.

If you hunt mule deer long enough, you'll face some trying times. It's a rare hunter who hasn't felt discouraged at some point, who hasn't been fatigued to the point of dropping, who hasn't missed an unmissable shot and sworn he'd quit hunting, who hasn't sat under a bush, soaked to the skin, hating his situation, hating himself. Mountain country can breed its own weather, and you can expect to get hit with violent thunderstorms, prolonged rain, nagging wind, blinding fog. Name some form of merciless weather, and you'll sooner or later get it hunting mule deer.

Along with that you'll walk many long miles, you'll get hungry, you'll have to operate on too little sleep. The list goes on. Things like this play as big a part in western hunting as blue skies, sunshine, soft breezes and big bucks.

It's one thing to sit in your living room making plans, dreaming about the wilderness life as mountain man on the last frontier. It's another to be out there with the wind tearing at your nerves like a dog shaking your pants leg, the sun shriveling your skin like bacon in a hot pan, the miles passing beneath your feet, each step draining your reservoir of energy. Under the stress of reality, you can end up hating the very country you love. Tough times can break your resolve and ruin a hunt. Unless you're ready.

A POSITIVE NOTE

Listing all the bad points about hunting might seem like a sour way to end a book, but I don't think that's really true. In fact, I don't even perceive tough elements as bad. They're just part of all hunting, and whether you see them as good or bad depends on our outlook.

As gung-ho teenagers many years ago, friends and I used to say the quality of a trip was proportional to the amount of suffering. Actually I think we said that then to justify the suffering we endured as a result of ill planning, but in a way that philosophy holds some wisdom, too. In all reality, shooting deer comprises a very small part of hunting. Statistics from various states show that bowhunters spend anywhere from 25 to 40 days in the field for every deer killed. That means they spend a lot of time out there doing something besides killing deer, and learning to appreciate

Western hunting involves far more than blue skies, sunshine, soft breezes and big bucks. Just ask Larry Jones. This picture was taken in sunny Arizona. At this point the sunshine is falling in liquid form, and Larry is desperately trying to dry his gloves over a smouldering fire.

all aspects of a hunt, not just the thrill of taking a deer, can magnify your hunting pleasure. Anyone can feel happy when he's tying his tag on a deer. It's what you do with all the other times that ranks you as a hunter.

Don't get me wrong. I'm not one who says that just being out there is good enough and the kill is secondary. In many cases that's a copout, a rationalization for failure. I'm out there to kill a deer, pure and simply. At the same time, I think it's crazy to let the outcome of a hunt ride on that one goal. Conditions might prevent your scoring despite your best efforts, but you can still have a great hunt.

PREPARING

With the right gear, you can mitigate the effects of wind and rain and snow so they're little more than a nuisance, and if you're in good shape, you can handle the physical strain. Going prepared gets you started right, but that's not the total answer for the enjoyment of tough hunting. Some hunters with the best of gear and conditioning still turn tail and run or mope around camp when things don't go just right.

One time my friend Mike Cupell said something that has stuck with me for many years.

"People have a bad time because their expectations are wrong," he said. "They expect one thing and when they get something else, they're disappointed. Things are ruined. I try never to go into any hunt with preconceived notions about how it should be. Then I'm never

The right gear can mitigate the effects of bad weather. With a comfortable camp and good raingear, foul weather is little more than a nuisance. Yet even some well-prepared hunters can't take it because they're not mentally prepared.

disappointed."

If you go into a hunt thinking it's going to be nothing but pleasure and good companionship and skinning out deer, you're only setting yourself up for disappointment. Too many variables can enter the picture. And if you view the trials of a hunt, the cold and wind and tiredness and failure as unpleasant, then you'll experience many bad trips. These things really don't mean anything in themselves. They're neutral. It's what you do with them that counts. Outdoors appreciation goes beyond gratification of the senses.

DON'T GIVE UP

For me outdoors pursuits become a personal test, an examination of my drive, perseverance and character. As I've said, I'm out there to kill an animal, sure enough, but for me no hunt is ever considered unsuccessful, even when I fail to kill a deer, as long as I pass the test of character.

One day out in the Oregon desert, a harsh land that can test your stamina better than any other, particularly stands out in my mind. It was not the first day of the hunt but the last. It had been a long hard hunt as I'd spent eight days hiking long miles up and down cliffs and rims. I was tired. I'd seen plenty of game and had had my chances to take deer, but it was one of those hunts where things just never seemed to jell, and my game bags were still rolled neatly in my pack. This last day had to count, or I'd face a long winter without venison.

My hopes were high as I sat on a long rim and scanned beautiful miles of broken canyon containing pockets of mountain mahogany and sagebrush. Surely I would see the deer of my dreams feeding here today. I'd tried hard and hadn't quit. My reward would come.

About 9 o'clock, before I'd spotted any bucks, puffy clouds began to form near the desert floor below, and then they shot upwards through the cliffs, driven by violent winds, like sheets flapping on a clothesline, and they billowed around to envelope me in a vast white pall. I couldn't see 50 yards. Deer spotting was out. For two hours I stewed and fretted. Certainly it would do no good, but I felt an urgency. Time was slipping away.

About noon the clouds evaporated as fast as they'd formed, and eagerly I started glassing again. But before I'd spotted an animal, thunder began to growl in the distance and grew nearer until it suddenly was crashing all around. Rain drops so huge and intense they hissed through the air like missiles splattered my clothing.

I ran down off the exposed rim and hunkered pitifully in a patch of scrub aspen, but I couldn't hide from the storm, and rain penetrated every crevice of my clothes. Even as I buried my head inside my shirt and squeezed my eyes tightly closed, lightning bolts flashed with blinding intensity, and with each flash, thunder instantly blasted surrounding ridges. A half-hour later, when the storm mercifully passed, I felt weak and empty. To compound that desperate feeling, a rising wind whipped through my soaked clothing and turned my skin to ice.

I tried to start a fire, but my matches were wet and every stick of firewood was soaked. I failed. It was stupid, getting caught ill-prepared like this, and I vowed right then never to get caught without a foolproof fire starter again. But at this moment that vow didn't do much good. I was freezing.

Shivering convulsively, I considered the hunt. The season would close in a few short hours, and chances for killing a deer now were slim, maybe zero. Why not head in? I'd given it a good shot. It was the only sensible thing to do.

I started walking back toward camp, but my feet dragged, and after a quarter-mile I stopped and turned back toward the canyons where I'd seen deer in the past, where my hopes lay for success.

"Don't quit," an inner voice whispered. "You've got a half-day left. Keep going. Don't quit!"

It seemed crazy but there still was time. It had happened before, and it could happen now. Walking had warmed me up and the wind, even freezing as it was, had begun to dry my clothes.

Heading back toward the hunting area, I nearly ran in anticipation. With renewed intensity I glassed and searched and, finally, late in the afternoon, I saw a buck, a 4-point, feeding in mahogany on a hillside a half-mile away. If I could only hurry there might be time for a shot.

The stalk took more than an hour, and night was coming on as I slipped the last few yards to gain a shooting position. But the deer wasn't there.

With binoculars I examined every twig and leaf for some sign of the buck. He'd vanished. The proverbial eleventh-hour buck had become a myth.

That ended the hunt. I hadn't killed a deer. I could have felt sad or frustrated, and surely I sensed some disappointment, but strangely I had no regrets that nine days of effort had come to naught. Did it matter that I hadn't killed a deer? Had the object of my efforts been a buck in the first place? Or had I myself been the object? Hadn't the hunt been simply a test? As I stumbled back to camp in the dark, still damp from the rain, cold in the swirling wind, I felt a warm glow of satisfaction, the kind a hunter feels only after a successful hunt. I hadn't quit. Wasn't that enough? That had been the object all along.

HIDDEN FEELINGS

Not only can mule deer hunting test your resolve, but it can bring out emotions and feelings you've forgot existed. I don't mean to dramatize hunting or to elevate it to a plane higher than it deserves. Some people try to make hunting into a mystical, almost religious experience, and I think that's all baloney. Nevertheless, tough hunting can test your spirit, and it can reach down to your guts as few other activities can to see what you're made of. In the workaday world, we live in a narrow emotional band and a sterile environment in which we exercise the same feelings and emotions day after day. I think sometimes life gets boring because we live in emotional monotony, and hunting serves a valuable function if for no other reason than it can break you out of that rut. To some people that's grossly unpleasant, and they're not prepared to deal with the trauma of change. To others, it's life itself.

One fall was especially hectic for me. My wife was due to have a baby, and I was trying to finish a book, and hunting had just about been squeezed out of the picture. Anyone who dreams hunting, as I do, knows the desperate nature of that situation. At the last minute, in early September, a block of five days broke open somewhere between the baby and the book, and a quick hunt seemed possible.

I took off for a place in Oregon's Blue Mountains I'd wanted to hunt for years. It held all the rugged beauty I'd remembered, and it contained the deer and other game. The first morning I saw a bull elk bugling, and another morning I watched a bear eating manzanita berries. I had plenty of chances to kill deer, but I just couldn't put everything together.

Storm after storm blew in to dump first rain, and then hail followed by snow, and the wind blew and then the fog rolled in, and it seemed like it was just one constant procession of terrible weather. To make things worse, I'd had little time that summer to get in shape, and the steep mountains were taking a toll, and I could feel the effects of the strain. One day I'd set down my pack to stalk a buck, and when I returned I couldn't find the pack. I climbed up and down, looking under a dozen trees, and each fruitless step drained away valuable energy until I felt near the breaking point, like the wife who's cleaned the house, fought with the kids all day and burned the dinner, then had her husband ask if something was wrong.

The last day heavy fog smothered the entire mountain range, and rain drizzled steadily. For several hours I hiked and looked, but with visibility of less than 50 yards, I saw no animals. My clothes were soaked and wind blowing through them chilled me to the marrow. I hunted by force of habit and will power alone, not from desire.

At dark, glad the hunt was finally over, I dragged myself down the steep, black canyon to base camp. There the ground, trees, tent, the very air was soggy and lifeless and lonely. Night was blacker than the inside of a wood stove. I had no energy to build a fire nor to eat, only to peel off my sopping clothes and to sleep. "Isn't hunting fun?" I said, trying to be funny. But I wasn't in a humorous mood and couldn't laugh.

The next morning at 7 a.m. the sky was clear. I built a huge fire that sent orange flames and sparks leaping 10 feet into the air, and I ate all my remaining food and dried my clothes. As I hit the trail to go home, sunlight filtered through the dense canopy of branches and sparkled off heavy frost on the grass. Near the creek it struck me — the cottonwood leaves had just turned gold. A light breeze tousled the limbs and big leaves, brilliant yellow against the blue sky, fluttered and spun overhead. Laying my pack aside, I flopped to my belly by the creek and sucked in a draught of pure water. My wool shirt soaked up the sun's warmth as a paper towel soaks up spilled milk and the heat felt good. I lay still for

Larry watches as fog builds up in a valley below and works its way up the mountain. When you get caught in fog you can do little more than twiddle your thumbs. How would you handle a situation like that? The success of your hunt rests on your reactions.

many minutes, thinking, and the harsh feelings I'd experience over the past few days seemed only distant, vague memories. Had it really rained? Had camp been dark and lonely? Had I been tired and hungry? Had I really blown shots at deer?

Sometimes during a rough trip I question whether I even like to hunt, but at the end I've never questioned whether I like having hunted. Psychologists say we forget the bad and remember the good, and maybe that was the mechanism at work in me then, but I think it went much deeper than that. This hunt had revived many feelings and emotions that had died in me over the years. During those five days a part of me that had been dead had been brought back to life. This hadn't been a hunt. It was a resurrection, and I felt good. Alive.

If it had been possible, I'd have turned around, gone back in to stay another day, another week. That was out of the question, though, because responsibility called me home. But even as my feet plodded grudgingly toward the car, my mind was at work, planning next year's hunt. This experience had changed my life, and I had to have more. That's the way it is, this bowhunting for mule deer.

CHAPTER 14

ONE LAST SHOT

Many hunters take good bow seasons for granted. In Wisconsin, for example, the bow season runs for 85 days and the gun season nine. I asked a big game specialist in Wisconsin when the Department of Natural Resources would trim off some of that season because it seemed so outrageously generous. Surely gun hunters wouldn't tolerate that for long.

"Oh, we think the long bow season is great," he said. "It provides a lot of hunting opportunity."

Except among bowhunters, that attitude doesn't prevail in the West. It seems like ranchers, farmers, rifle hunters, public land agencies, many members of wildlife commissions, and even some biologists view bowhunting with suspicion, and they allow bow seasons grudgingly, only because of demand, not because they think bowhunting has any merit.

Sadly, the setting of regulations often comes down to a war between rifle and bow hunters, rather than a unified attempt by hunters to support the greatest possible hunting opportunity. Many detractors say, "Why should bow seasons be longer than rifle seasons? It's not fair." Sadly, some bow seasons are set on that very reasoning, and biological data, harvest statistics and common sense be hanged. Of course, shorter bow seasons don't mean longer rifle seasons, so a reduction just to placate irate rifle hunters or others who don't like bowhunting means nobody gains and everybody loses.

Generous bow seasons don't just happen. Someone has fought for those seasons, and we all should support that effort. Recently the Oregon wildlife department held a public hearing in my hometown to hear hunters' opinions on the upcoming seasons. Exactly one person signed up to testify. Me. Where the devil was everybody else? When hunters do nothing, commissioners do what they very well please. And often it's not in the best interest of bowhunting.

One time a Californian wrote to me and asked how he could join the Oregon Bow Hunters. He liked to hunt in Oregon and he wanted to support the organization that had fought for Oregon's good bow seasons. That guy was on the right track. He didn't just sit back and take advantage of a good situation someone else had created. If you like to hunt a particular state, support local groups that fight for your seasons.

Do whatever you can to get the rotten apples out the bowhunter's barrel, too. In recent years all western states have established poaching hotlines, toll-free numbers on which game-law violations can be reported anonymously so you can easily report violations. In Wyoming, one woman reported her own husband for poaching deer. Good for her. It's time some of us got angry enough to do something besides look the other way. Maybe you don't feel the urgency, and a lot of hunters don't. But I think it's a significant issue and could affect the future of western bowhunting.

This all sounds real high minded, watching others and cleaning their house for them, and it's something we must do if we want to keep bowhunting. But it's not the place to start. The starting point is ourselves. One year while hunting the desert I noticed a buck hanging in the camp next to my camp. A young boy maybe 14 or 15 years old sat in camp by himself, so I wandered over to chat.

"Nice buck," I said. "Who got him?"

"I did," the boy replied.

"That's great," I said. "Took me a lot of years to kill a buck like that. You're off to a good start. How'd you get him?"

The boy described in detail how he'd spotted the deer from a distance and had sneaked within range and had made a clean, killing shot. I was impressed. He'd obviously had a good teacher.

The next day I met another man who knew the boy and his father. I said to the man, "Did you see the buck that young boy shot?"

He laughed. "Are you kidding? That kid didn't shoot any deer. His dad shot it and had the boy tag it so he could keep on hunting."

That ranks as one of the saddest experiences of my hunting life. Not only had that family flagrantly broken the law — in all western states shooting game for someone else is illegal — but the father had taught his son to lie. And very well at that.If that were an isolated example, I'd probably brush it aside as insignificant, nothing more than an example of one renegade family, but sadly, it symbolizes a common attitude. Many hunters, and not just malcontents but so-called respected citizens, too, brag about taking over-limits and filling tags for others.

These people not only destroy the ethical fiber of those around them, but they jeopardize the future of hunting for everyone. We hear repeatedly about the problems facing the future of deer hunting — land development, loss of winter range, poaching, road kills — and these are critical. Hunters must serve as watchdogs for the future of big game and actively shape that future. But I think it's a hollow voice that thunders for better land use, or decries the actions of poachers, and then whispers, "I filled my wife's tag today." That's the attitude that could destroy bowhunting in the West.

Since 1974, bowhunting success nationwide has risen from about 5 percent to 11 percent. The American Archery Council recently surveyed more than 3,000 bowhunters to ask, "What do you think has contributed most to the increased success?"

The No. 1 answer was "better hunting knowledge." Bowhunters today know far more about hunting than they did even 10 years ago. With proliferating magazine articles, books, tape recordings, video tapes, seminars and so forth, the modern bowhunter can learn how to hunt before he sets foot out the door, and those of us who disseminate the information unquestionably help shape the future of the sport. Bow seasons are generous because bowhunting is a low-kill sport. When we get too good, we threaten our own well-being.

For that reason, I sometimes hesitate even to write about hunting, because my writing then contributes to the rising success. When I first started elk hunting, for example, few bowhunters really knew much about elk. It took me four years of trial and error to put everything together to kill an elk, and few other hunters were doing much better. Any guy who'd bugled in and killed more than one or two elk at that time was regarded as a living legend.

Since then bugling has caught on. After finally learning something about the subject myself, I wrote a book called, *Bugling for Elk*, and many hunters have written to me recently saying they read my book, followed my advice, and killed bulls their first time out.

In a way I'm flattered because it means I wrote the truth and others profitted from my knowledge, and helping others makes me feel good. At the same time, it gives me an ominous sense of responsibility, because I know some hunters could abuse that knowledge and jeopardize the future of bowhunting, the very thing I'm trying to promote.

I hope you take this book — and any other material that helps you become a better hunter — and apply it in the field. If you practice my ideas, I guarantee you'll kill deer. At the same time I hope you'll practice restraint. Each of us must play a personal role in fighting for the best of bowhunting, and the place to start is with ourselves. Anybody can kill more than his share of the deer; it doesn't take a man to do that. The real man is the one who could do it. And doesn't.

THE END

APPENDIX 1

PLANNING AIDS

The addresses here will get you started in planning. These are major offices for each state and region, and from these you can get the addresses and phone numbers for all lower offices.

STATE WILDLIFE OFFICES

From state wildlife agencies you can obtain current hunting regulations, information sources such as the names of biologists, maps of state-owned hunting lands, and in most cases, a list of guides and outfitters in that state.

Game and Fish Department
2222 W. Greenway Rd.
Phoenix, AZ 85023
(602) 942-3000

Division of Wildlife
6060 Broadway
Denver, CO 80216
(303) 825-1192

Fish and Game Department
600 S. Walnut
P.O. Box 25
Boise, ID 83707
(208) 334-3700

Department of Fish, Wildlife and Parks
1420 E. Sixth
Helena, MT 59601
(406) 449-2535

Game and Fish Department
Villagra Building
Santa Fe, NM 87503
(505) 827-2923

Department of Fish & Wildlife
P.O. Box 3503
Portland, OR 97208
(503) 229-5551

Division of Wildlife Resources
1596 W.N. Temple
Salt Lake City, UT 84116
(801) 533-9333

Department of Game
600 N. Capitol Way
Olympia, WA 98504
(206) 753-5700

Game and Fish Department
Cheyenne, Wy 82002
(307) 777-7631

Energy & Natural Resources
Fish & Wildlife Division
Main Floor, North Tower
Petroleum Plasa
9945-108 Street
Edmonton, AB T5K 2C6
(403) 427-6750

Fish and Wildlife Branch
Ministry of Environment
Parliament Buildings
Victoria, B.C. V8V 1X4
(604) 387-5921

U.S. FOREST SERVICE

From these central offices you can get a complete list of National Forests for each region. There is a nominal cost for these maps.

Region 1 (Montana, Northern Idaho)
Federal Building
Missoula, MT 89807
(406) 329-3316

Region 2 (Colorado, part of Wyoming)
11177 W. 8th Ave.
P.O. Box 25127
Lakewood, CO 80225
(303) 234-3711

Region 3 (Arizona, New Mexico)
Federal Building
517 Gold Ave. S.W.
Albuquerque, NM 87102
(505) 766-2401

Region 4 (Nevada, Utah, Southern Idaho, Western Wyoming)
Federal Building
324 25th St.
Ogden, UT 84401
(801) 626-3201

Region 5 (California)
630 Sansome St.
San Francisco, CA 94111
(415) 556-4310

Region 6 (Oregon, Washington)
319 S.W. Pine St.
P.O. Box 3623
Portland, OR 97208
(503) 221-3625

BUREAU OF LAND MANAGEMENT

Ask for a free State Index Map. These list all BLM maps for each state. Prices vary but most maps cost about $2. For free Index Maps, write to Bureau of Land Management, State Office at the following addresses:

2400 Valley Bank Center
Phoenix, AZ 85073
(602) 261-3873

Federal Building, Room E-2841
2800 Cottage Way
Sacramento, CA 95825
(916) 484-4676

Colorado State Bank Building
1600 Broadway
Denver, CO 80202
(303) 837-4325

398 Federal Building
550 W. Fort St.
Boise, ID 83724
(208) 384-1401

222 N. 32nd St.
P.O. Box 30157
Billings, MT 59107
(406) 657-6462

Federal Building. Room 3008
300 Booth St.
Reno, NV 89509
(702) 784-5451

Federal Building
South Federal Place
Santa Fe. NM 87501
(505) 988-6217

(Oregon and Washington)
729 N.E. Oregon St.
P.O. Box 2965
Portland, OR 97208
(503) 231-6281

University Club Building
136 S. Temple
Salt Lake City, UT 84111
(801) 524-5311

2515 Warren Ave.
P.O. Box 1828
Cheyenne, WY 82001
(307) 778-2326

TOPOGRAPHIC MAPS

First ask for free state order maps, then from those order the specific state, regional, county or quadrangle topographic maps to cover your hunting areas.

Branch of Distribution
U.S. Geological Survey
Federal Center
Denver, CO 80225
(303) 234-3832

BOOKS TO AID YOUR PLANNING

An invaluable source of information sources is the *CONSERVATION DIRECTORY*. It lists addresses, phone numbers and the names of contacts in all state and provincial wildlife agencies; offices for federal land management agencies; private conservation groups throughout North America, and much more. This book is a must for anyone seriously planning a hunt. Contact:

National Wildlife Federation
1412 Sixteenth St., N.W.
Washington, D.C. 20036
(202) 797-6800

The best book written strictly on mule deer hunting (next to the one you're reading, of course) is *HOW TO FIND GIANT BUCKS* by Kirt Darner. This book isn't on bowhunting, but it's on trophy mule deer hunting, and Darner's tips on researching hunting areas, and his one chapter, "Where to find Record Class Bucks Today," by themselves are worth the price of the book. Send $22 (price includes postage) to:

Kirt Darner
P.O. Box 1606
Montrose, CO 81402

MULE AND BLACK-TAILED DEER   OF 'NORTH AMERICA , a Wildlife Management Institute book compiled and edited by Olof C. Wallmo, provides a wealth of biological data of in terest to serious mule deer hunters. Contact:

University of Nebraska Press
901 North 17th Street
Lincoln, NE 68588

Official record books are invaluable sources of information. To find out where the biggest bucks grow, study Boone and Crockett's RECORDS OF NORTH AMERICAN BIG GAME, the official Boone and Crockett record book. A recent edition, 18th BIG GAME AWARDS, also shows some tremendous bucks and tells the stories behind bucks entered during a recent scoring period, 1980-1982. For information on these books, contact:

Boone and Crockett Club
205 S. Patrick St.
Alexandria, VA 22314
(703) 548-7727

The Pope and Young Club's BOWHUNTING BIG GAME RECORDS OF NORTH AMERICA, also contains plenty of good information and data that tell where bowhunters have taken the biggest bucks. For information on this book, contact:

Pope and Young Club
6471 Richard Ave.
Placerville, CA 95667
(916) 621-1133

HUNTING AMERICA'S MULE DEER by Jim Zumbo is not a bowhunting book but it contains good general information about different kinds of mule deer habitat around the West and can help give you a picture of the country. To order, write:

Jim Zumbo
P.O. Box 1077
Vernal, UT 84078

COLORADO'S BIGGEST BUCKS AND BULLS by Jack and Susan Reneau, contains some good information on where to find trophy bucks in Colorado. For more information, write to:

Jack and Susan Reneau
13506 Kingsman Road
Woodbridge, VA 22193

APPENDIX 2

LEARNING TO SHOOT A BOW

Preventing bad habits is a lot easier than unlearning them, so work on basics before taking to the field. The ideal is to take lessons from a professional instructor, but if that's not possible, follow these tips. This is written for right-handed shooters, so lefties do the opposite. Most of the following tips come from Lonnie Jones, a professional archery instructor.

Stand close to the target and place your feet at a 90-degree angle to the target, then step back about 6 inches with the forward foot and pivot slightly toward the target. This gives you a slightly open stance.

Now place your hands correctly. Your bow (left) hand should assume a natural position, turned slightly inward. To see what I mean, hold it up without the bow as if you're pointing at a distant mountain. Your hand will be turned, not straight up and down, and that's the way it should be on the bow. With your hand correctly on the bow handle, your little finger will be to the side of the bow, not in front. If you force your hand vertical so all your fingers are in line with the bow, your hand will torque the bow during a shot and throw the arrow off. The bow hand should rest solidly on the fleshy part of the thumb with maximum pressure about 1 inch above the big thumb knuckle, and bow-hand fingers should hang limply. Don't squeeze the bow or extend your fingers stiffly.

Position the index finger of your right hand above the arrow and the middle and fourth fingers below the arrow; the string should lay about half-way between the first knuckle and the tips of the fingers. This hand, too, should be rotated slightly inward in a natural position. With your bow arm and right wrist straight, raise the entire bow-and-arm unit until you're aiming at the target. As you begin to draw, concentrate on pushing back the right elbow, which forces you to pull with strong back muscles. If you focus on the string you'll pull with the bicep, which is a relatively weak muscle. Draw to your anchor point, a fixed position to which you draw every time. A common anchor point is the tip of the index finger at the corner of the mouth, although some archers anchor with the middle

Professional instructor Lonnie Jones demonstrates good shooting form. Notice in particular that his bowhand is relaxed and held in a natural position. The little finger is not forced in front of the bow. The string hand also is turned slightly in a natural position. With eyes closed, Jones can forget about hitting the target to concentrate on form.

finger at the corner of the mouth, and others, particularly target archers, anchor with the thumb under the chin.

To shoot, let the string slip from your fingers. Don't deliberately release by throwing open your hand or jerking your hand back; that will throw off the shot. Simply let the string hand relax and the string will suddenly be gone. After the shot this hand should be relaxed, right beside your cheek. As Lonnie Jones said: "Don't let go of the string; let the string go." After the shot continue to aim at the target. Your bow should not have moved. Continuing to aim after the shot is commonly called "follow through."

Lonnie Jones emphasizes that proper alignment and relaxation underlie all good shooting. Muscle tension forces you into unnatural positions and will throw off a shot. Jones suggests practicing with your eyes closed to develop good form and relaxation. Stand about 10 feet from the target to assure that you don't miss, then follow these steps:

1. Assume a slightly open stance as described above.

2. Set your bow hand, rotated slightly inward, with maximum pressure about 1 inch above the big thumb joint.

3. Place the index finger of your right hand above the arrow and the middle and fourth fingers below. The string hand is rotated slightly inward and the wrist is straight.

4. Raise the entire bow-and-arm unit to shooting position and aim at the target.

5. Now close your eyes. This allows you to forget about aiming so you can concentrate solely on shooting form. With eyes closed run through these check points:

6. Push back the right elbow until you've reached your anchor point.

7. Switch concentration to your bow hand. Are the fingers totally limp? This check point is critical. From start to finish of a shot the bow fingers must be relaxed. Tense fingers indicate muscle tension elsewhere that can throw off a shot.

8. Now let the string hand relax and the string will slip away.

9. Keep your eyes closed. Is the draw hand hanging limply beside your cheek? Is your bow hand still loose and relaxed?

10. Now open your eyes. Are you still on target? Even with eyes closed, you should have hit right where you aimed, and you should be able to shoot a tight group, which indicates consistent form.

Develop good, relaxed form first, and then practice for hunting by roving, shooting small game and shooting in tournaments.

APPENDIX 3
HUNTING GEAR

Equipment can make or break a hunting trip, so plan for every contingency. I carry the hunting-pack items in a small fanny pack, and it goes with me whenever I'm in the field. For general camping I've listed only backpacking equipment because backpacking serves as the lowest common denominator; it involves the minimum of equipment mandatory for any hunt. For car or horse camping I'd take the same basic equipment only in greater quantity and size.

My hunting pack always includes these items:

1. Flashlight (one battery turned backwards to prevent draining the batteries; spare batteries; spare bulb.)
2. Map and compass.
3. Fire-starting materials (matches, butane lighter, pitch wood.)
4. 1 mil plastic tarp for emergency shelter.
5. Knife.
6. Sharpening stone or small steel.
7. First aid kit (bandaids, gauze, aspirin, moleskin.)
8. 50 feet of nylon cord.
9. Whistle (for emergency signalling.)
10. Plastic flagging (for marking trail to and from meat, etc.)
11. Three feet of surgical tubing and cup for siphoning water.
12. Lunch and high-energy foods.
13. At times my hunting pack also might include raingear, extra eye glasses, water bottle, camera and film, wool shirt or down vest, folding saw.

For bivouac hunting I would stuff the following items into a rucksack to carry in addition to the above items:

1. 2-pound down sleeping bag.
2. Bivvy sack for shelter.
3. Soap and wash cloth.
4. Tooth brush.
5. Small aluminum pot.
6. Spoon.
7. Gasoline or sterno stove.
8. Sock hat (to keep warm while sleeping.)
9. About 1 pound of food per day.

Following is a list of items I'd take on the average backpack hunting trip:

1. Spotting scope.
2. Binoculars.
3. Rope for camp use.
4. Camouflage face paint.
5 Bow with 1 dozen hunting arrows and 5 practice arrows.
6. Extra pre-sharpened broadheads.
7. Finger tab and arm guard.
8. Extra bow string.
9. Bow string wax.
10. Extra arrow rest for bow.
11. Hunting boots or shoes and light shoes for camp wear.
12. Socks — 3 pairs light, 3 pairs heavy wool.
13. 2 t-shirts.

14. 2 underwear.
15. 3 hankies.
16. Wool shirt and pants.
17. Cotton camouflage shirt and pants (in predictably hot situations.)
18. Wool gloves.
19. Camouflage hat.
20. Wool sock hat.
21. Down jacket for camp use.
22. Wool scarf.
23. Raingear.
24. Two-man tent.
25. Nylon or plastic tarp for lean-to shelter.
26. Foam sleeping pad.
27. Sleeping bag.
28. Gasoline stove.
29. Matches.
30. Quart pot and handle.
31. Fork, cup and plate.
32. Dish cloth and soap.
33. Alarm clock (wrist alarm chronograph.)
34. Assorted plastic bags.
35. Towel and soap.
36. Nylon twine for general camp use.
37. Notebook and pens.
38. Toothbrush and paste.
39. Toilet paper.
40. Sweat band.
41. Comb.
42. Thermometer (for checking meat temperature.)
43. Flashlight for camp use.
44. Packframe and packsack.
45. Extra pins and keepers for packframe.
46. Candles for light in tent.
47. Leader and hooks for fishing.
48. Camera, lenses, film.
49. Food (My backpacking menu generally includes granola or oatmeal cereal for breakfast; hard rolls or flour tortillas, cheese, dried beef for lunch; Mountain House freeze-dried dinners for dinner; plus gorp — raisins, nuts, chocolate candies — and jerky for snacking food during the day.)

MEASURING TROPHIES

We gratefully acknowledge permission from the Boone and Crockett Club through its executive director, Wm. H. Nesbitt, for permission to reproduce the following Boone and Crockett Club score charts.

Minimum Score:
whitetail 170
Coues' 110

TYPICAL
WHITETAIL AND COUES' DEER

Kind of Deer_____

DETAIL OF POINT MEASUREMENT

	Abnormal Points	
	Right	Left
	Total to E	

SEE OTHER SIDE FOR INSTRUCTIONS			Column 1	Column 2	Column 3	Column 4
	R.	L.	Spread Credit	Right Antler	Left Antler	Difference
A. Number of Points on Each Antler						
B. Tip to Tip Spread						
C. Greatest Spread						
D. Inside Spread of Main Beams — Credit may equal but not exceed length of longer antler. IF Spread exceeds longer antler, enter difference.						
E. Total of Lengths of all Abnormal Points						
F. Length of Main Beam						
G-1. Length of First Point, if present						
G-2. Length of Second Point						
G-3. Length of Third Point						
G-4. Length of Fourth Point, if present						
G-5. Length of Fifth Point, if present						
G-6. Length of Sixth Point, if present						
G-7. Length of Seventh Point, if present						
H-1. Circumference at Smallest Place Between Burr and First Point						
H-2. Circumference at Smallest Place Between First and Second Points						
H-3. Circumference at Smallest Place Between Second and Third Points						
H-4. Circumference at Smallest Place between Third and Fourth Points (see back if G-4 is missing)						
TOTALS						

ADD	Column 1		Exact locality where killed
	Column 2		Date killed By whom killed
	Column 3		Present owner
	Total		Address
SUBTRACT Column 4			Guide's Name and Address
FINAL SCORE			Remarks: (Mention any abnormalities or unique qualities)

I certify that I have measured the above trophy on _____ 19_____
at (address) _____
                                               City   State
and that these measurements and data are, to the best of my knowledge and belief, made in accordance with the instructions given.

Witness: _____ Signature: _____

OFFICIAL MEASURER | | | | |

INSTRUCTIONS FOR MEASURING WHITETAIL AND COUES' DEER

All measurements must be made with a ¼-inch flexible steel tape to the nearest one-eighth of an inch. Wherever it is necessary to change direction of measurement, mark a control point and swing tape at this point. Enter fractional figures in eighths, without reduction. Official measurements cannot be taken for at least sixty days after the animal was killed.

A. Number of Points on Each Antler. To be counted a point, a projection must be at least one inch long and its length must exceed the width of its base. All points are measured from tip of point to nearest edge of beam as illustrated. Beam tip is counted as a point but not measured as a point.

B. Tip to Tip Spread is measured between tips of main beams.

C. Greatest Spread is measured between perpendiculars at a right angle to the center line of the skull at widest part whether across main beams or points.

D. Inside Spread of Main Beams is measured at a right angle to the center line of the skull at widest point between main beams. Enter this measurement again in Spread Credit column if it is less than or equal to the length of longer antler; if longer, enter longer antler length for Spread Credit.

E. Total of lengths of all Abnormal Points. Abnormal points are those nontypical in location (points originating from points or from sides or bottom of main beam) or extra points beyond the normal pattern of up to eight normal points, including beam tip, per antler. Measure in usual manner and enter in appropriate blanks.

F. Length of Main Beam is measured from lowest outside edge of burr over outer curve to the most distant point of what is, or appears to be, the main beam. The point of beginning is that point on the burr where the center line along the outer curve of the beam intersects the burr, then following generally the line of the illustration.

G-1-2-3-4-5-6-7. Length of Normal Points. Normal points project from the top of the main beam. They are measured from nearest edge of main beam over outer curve to tip. Lay the tape along the outer curve of the beam so that the top edge of the tape coincides with the top edge of the beam on both sides of the point to determine baseline for point measurements. Record point lengths in appropriate blanks.

H-1-2-3-4. Circumferences are taken as detailed for each measurement. If brow point is missing, take H-1 and H-2 at smallest place between burr and G-2. If G-4 is missing, take H-4 halfway between G-3 and tip of main beam.

* * * * * * * * * * * *

FAIR CHASE STATEMENT FOR ALL HUNTER-TAKEN TROPHIES

To make use of the following methods shall be deemed as UNFAIR CHASE and unsportsmanlike, and any trophy obtained by use of such means is disqualified from entry for Awards.
    I. Spotting or herding game from the air, followed by landing in its vicinity for pursuit;
   II. Herding or pursuing game with motor-powered vehicles;
  III. Use of electronic communications for attracting, locating or observing game, or guiding the hunter to such game;
   IV. Hunting game confined by artificial barriers, including escape-proof fencing; or hunting game transplanted solely for the purpose of commercial shooting.

****

I certify that the trophy scored on this chart was not taken in UNFAIR CHASE as defined above by the Boone and Crockett Club. I further certify that it was taken in full compliance with local game laws of the state, province, or territory.

Date_____ Signature of Hunter_____
(Have signature notarized by a Notary Public)

OFFICIAL SCORING SYSTEM FOR NORTH AMERICAN BIG GAME TROPHIES

Records of North American
Big Game

BOONE AND CROCKETT CLUB

205 South Patrick Street
Alexandria, Virginia 22314

Minimum Score:
whitetail 195
Coues' 120

NON-TYPICAL
WHITETAIL AND COUES' DEER

Kind of Deer_____

DETAIL OF POINT MEASUREMENT

Abnormal Points	
Right	Left
Total to E	

SEE OTHER SIDE FOR INSTRUCTIONS		R.	L.	Column 1	Column 2	Column 3	Column 4
				Spread Credit	Right Antler	Left Antler	Difference
A.	Number of Points on Each Antler						
B.	Tip to Tip Spread						
C.	Greatest Spread						
D.	Inside Spread of Main Beams	Credit may equal but not exceed length of longer antler					
IF Spread exceeds longer antler, enter difference.							
E.	Total of Lengths of Abnormal Points						
F.	Length of Main Beam						
G-1.	Length of First Point, if present						
G-2.	Length of Second Point						
G-3.	Length of Third Point						
G-4.	Length of Fourth Point, if present						
G-5.	Length of Fifth Point, if present						
G-6.	Length of Sixth Point, if present						
G-7.	Length of Seventh Point, if present						
H-1.	Circumference at Smallest Place Between Burr and First Point						
H-2.	Circumference at Smallest Place Between First and Second Points						
H-3.	Circumference at Smallest Place Between Second and Third Points						
H-4.	Circumference at Smallest Place Between Third and Fourth Points						
	TOTALS						

ADD	Column 1		Exact locality where killed
	Column 2		Date killed By whom killed
	Column 3		Present owner
SUBTRACT	Total		Address
	Column 4		
	Result		Guide's Name and Address
Add line E Total			Remarks: (Mention any abnormalities or unique qualities)
FINAL SCORE			

I certify that I have measured the above trophy on _____ 19 _____
at (address) _____ State_____ .
                                                  City
and that these measurements and data are, to the best of my knowledge and belief, made in accordance
with the instructions given.

Witness: _____ Signature: _____
                                                           OFFICIAL MEASURER

INSTRUCTIONS FOR MEASURING NON-TYPICAL WHITETAIL AND COUES' DEER

All measurements must be made with a ¼-inch flexible steel tape to the nearest one-eighth of an inch.
Wherever it is necessary to change direction of measurement, mark a control point and swing tape at
this point. Enter fractional figures in eighths, without reduction. Official measurements cannot
be taken for at least sixty days after the animal was killed.

A. Number of Points on Each Antler. To be counted a point, a projection must be at least one inch
long and its length must exceed the width of its base. All points are measured from tip of point to
nearest edge of beam as illustrated. Beam tip is counted as a point but not measured as a point.

B. Tip to Tip Spread is measured between tips of main beams.

C. Greatest Spread is measured between perpendiculars at a right angle to the center line of the
skull at widest part whether across main beams or points.

D. Inside Spread of Main Beams is measured at a right angle to the center line of the skull at widest point between main beams. Enter this measurement again in Spread Credit column if it is less
than or equal to the length of longer antler; if longer, enter longer antler length for Spread Credit.

E. Total of Lengths of all Abnormal Points. Abnormal points are those nontypical in location (points
originating from points or from sides or bottom of main beam) or extra points beyond the normal pattern
of up to eight normal points, including beam tip, per antler. Measure in usual manner and enter in
appropriate blanks.

F. Length of Main Beam is measured from lowest outside edge of burr over outer curve to the most distant point of what is, or appears to be, the main beam. The point of beginning is that point on the
burr where the center line along the outer curve of the beam intersects the burr, then following generally the line of the illustration.

G-1-2-3-4-5-6-7. Length of Normal Points. Normal points project from the top of the main beam.
They are measured from nearest edge of main beam over outer curve to tip. Lay the tape along the
outer curve of the beam so that the top edge of the tape coincides with the beam on both sides of
the point to determine baseline for point measurement. Record point lengths in appropriate blanks.

H-1-2-3-4. Circumferences are taken as detailed for each measurement. If brow point is missing,
take H-1 and H-2 at smallest place between burr and G-2. If G-4 is missing, take H-4 halfway between
G-3 and tip of main beam.

* * * * * * * * * * * *
FAIR CHASE STATEMENT FOR ALL HUNTER-TAKEN TROPHIES
To make use of the following methods shall be deemed as UNFAIR CHASE and unsportsmanlike, and any
trophy obtained by use of such means is disqualified from entry for Awards.
    I. Spotting or herding game from the air, followed by landing in its vicinity
       for pursuit;
   II. Herding or pursuing game with motor-powered vehicles;
  III. Use of electronic communications for attracting, locating or observing
       game, or guiding the hunter to such game;
   IV. Hunting game confined by artificial barriers, including escape-proof fencing;
       or hunting game transplanted solely for the purpose of commercial shooting.
****
I certify that the trophy scored on this chart was not taken in UNFAIR CHASE as defined above by the
Boone and Crockett Club. I further certify that it was taken in full compliance with local game laws
of the state, province, or territory.
Date_____Signature of Hunter_____
(Have signature notarized by a Notary Public)

Records of North American
Big Game

BOONE AND CROCKETT CLUB

205 South Patrick Street
Alexandria, Virginia 22314

Minimum Score:
mule   195
blacktail 130

TYPICAL
MULE AND BLACKTAIL DEER

Kind of Deer _____

DETAIL OF POINT MEASUREMENT

	Abnormal Points	
	Right	Left
Total to E		

SEE OTHER SIDE FOR INSTRUCTIONS			Column 1	Column 2	Column 3	Column 4
		R.	L.	Spread Credit	Right Antler	Left Antler	Difference
A. Number of points on Each Antler							
B. Tip to Tip Spread							
C. Greatest Spread							
D. Inside Spread of Main Beams	Credit may equal but not exceed length of longer antler						
IF Spread exceeds longer antler, enter difference							
E. Total of Lengths of Abnormal Points							
F. Length of Main Beam							
G-1. Length of First Point, if present							
G-2. Length of Second Point							
G-3. Length of Third Point, if present							
G-4. Length of Fourth Point, if present							
H-1. Circumference at Smallest Place Between Burr and First Point							
H-2. Circumference at Smallest Place Between First and Second Points							
H-3. Circumference at Smallest Place Between Main Beam and Third Point							
H-4. Circumference at Smallest Place Between Second and Fourth Points							
TOTALS							

ADD	Column 1		Exact locality where killed
	Column 2		Date killed By whom killed
	Column 3		Present owner
TOTAL			Address
SUBTRACT Column 4			Guide's Name and Address
FINAL SCORE			Remarks: (Mention any abnormalities or unique qualities)

I certify that I have measured the above trophy on _____ 19_____
at (address) _____ _____
                                                 City   State
and that these measurements and data are, to the best of my knowledge and belief, made in accordance
with the instructions given.

Witness: _____ Signature: _____

                                                   OFFICIAL MEASURER

INSTRUCTIONS FOR MEASURING MULE AND BLACKTAIL DEER

All measurements must be made with a ¼-inch flexible steel tape to the nearest one-eighth of an inch.
Wherever it is necessary to change direction of measurement, mark a control point and swing tape at
this point. Enter fractional figures in eighths, without reduction. Official measurements cannot
be taken for at least sixty days after the animal was killed.

A. Number of Points on Each Antler. To be counted a point, a projection must be at least one inch
long and its length must exceed the width of its base. All points are measured from tip of point to
nearest edge of beam as illustrated. Beam tip is counted as a point but not measured as a point.

B. Tip to Tip Spread is measured between tips of main beams.

C. Greatest Spread is measured between perpendiculars at a right angle to the center line of the
skull at widest part whether across main beams or points.

D. Inside Spread of Main Beams is measured at a right angle to the center line of the skull at widest point between main beams. Enter this measurement again in Spread Credit column if it is less
than or equal to the length of longer antler; if longer, enter longer antler length for Spread Credit.

E. Total Lengths of all Abnormal Points. Abnormal points are those nontypical in location such as
points originating from a point (exception: G-3 originates from G-2 in perfectly normal fashion) or
from sides or bottom of main beam or any points beyond the normal pattern of five (including beam
tip) per antler. Measure each abnormal point in usual manner and enter in appropriate blanks.

F. Length of Main Beam is measured from lowest outside edge of burr over outer curve to the tip of
the main beam. The point of beginning is that point on the burr where the center line along the
outer curve of the beam intersects the burr, then following generally the line of the illustration.

G-1-2-3-4. Length of Normal Points. Normal points are the brow and the upper and lower forks as
shown in the illustration. They are measured from nearest edge of beam over outer curve to tip.
Lay the tape along the outer curve of the beam so that the top edge of the tape coincides with the
top edge of the beam on both sides of the point to determine baseline for point measurement. Record
point lengths in appropriate blanks.

H-1-2-3-4. Circumferences are taken as detailed for each measurement. If brow point is missing,
take H-1 and H-2 at smallest place between burr and G-2. If G-3 is missing, take H-3 halfway between
the base and tip of second point. If G-4 is missing, take H-4 halfway between the second point and
tip of main beam. * * * * * * * * * * * *

FAIR CHASE STATEMENT FOR ALL HUNTER-TAKEN TROPHIES

To make use of the following methods shall be deemed as UNFAIR CHASE and unsportsmanlike, and any
trophy obtained by use of such means is disqualified from entry for Awards.
    I.   Spotting or herding game from the air, followed by landing in its vicinity
        for pursuit;
   II.   Herding or pursuing game with motor-powered vehicles;
  III.   Use of electronic communications for attracting, locating or observing
        game, or guiding the hunter to such game;
   IV.   Hunting game confined by artificial barriers, including escape-proof fencing;
        or hunting game transplanted solely for the purpose of commercial shooting.
    ****
I certify that the trophy scored on this chart was not taken in UNFAIR CHASE as defined above by the
Boone and Crockett Club. I further certify that it was taken in full compliance with local game laws
of the state, province, or territory.
Date_____ Signature of Hunter_____
(Have signature notarized by a Notary Public)

Records of North American
Big Game

BOONE AND CROCKETT CLUB

205 South Patrick Street
Alexandria, Virginia 22314

Minimum Score: 240

NON-TYPICAL
MULE DEER

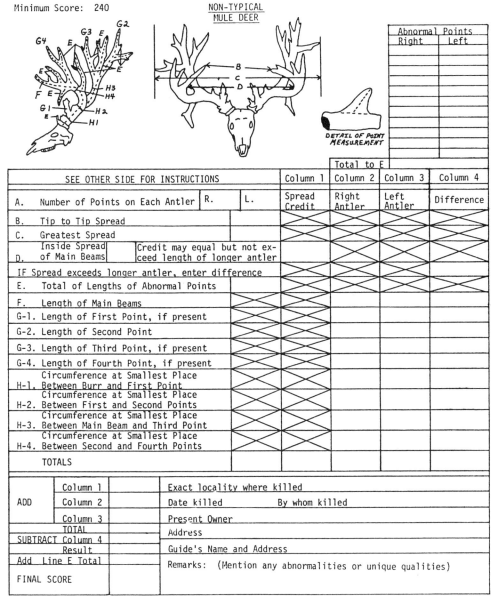

		Abnormal Points	
		Right	Left
		Total to E	

DETAIL OF POINT MEASUREMENT

SEE OTHER SIDE FOR INSTRUCTIONS			Column 1	Column 2	Column 3	Column 4
A. Number of Points on Each Antler	R.	L.	Spread Credit	Right Antler	Left Antler	Difference
B. Tip to Tip Spread						
C. Greatest Spread						
D. Inside Spread of Main Beams	Credit may equal but not exceed length of longer antler					
IF Spread exceeds longer antler, enter difference						
E. Total of Lengths of Abnormal Points						
F. Length of Main Beams						
G-1. Length of First Point, if present						
G-2. Length of Second Point						
G-3. Length of Third Point, if present						
G-4. Length of Fourth Point, if present						
H-1. Circumference at Smallest Place Between Burr and First Point						
H-2. Circumference at Smallest Place Between First and Second Points						
H-3. Circumference at Smallest Place Between Main Beam and Third Point						
H-4. Circumference at Smallest Place Between Second and Fourth Points						
TOTALS						

ADD	Column 1		Exact locality where killed
	Column 2		Date killed By whom killed
	Column 3		Present Owner
	TOTAL		Address
SUBTRACT Column 4			
	Result		Guide's Name and Address
Add Line E Total			Remarks: (Mention any abnormalities or unique qualities)
FINAL SCORE			

I certify that I have measured the above trophy on _____ 19_____
at (address) _____ City _____ State_____
and that these measurements and data are, to the best of my knowledge and belief, made in accordance
with the instructions given.

Witness: _____ Signature: _____

OFFICIAL MEASURER ⟮ ⟮ ⟮ ⟮ ⟯

INSTRUCTIONS FOR MEASURING NON-TYPICAL MULE DEER

All measurements must be made with a ¼-inch flexible steel tape to the nearest one-eighth of an inch.
Wherever it is necessary to change direction of measurement, mark a control point and swing tape at
this point. Enter fractional figures in eighths, without reduction. Official measurements cannot
be taken for at least sixty days after the animal was killed.

A. Number of Points on Each Antler. To be counted a point, a projection must be at least one inch
long and its length must exceed the width of its base. All points are measured from tip of point to
nearest edge of beam as illustrated. Beam tip is counted as a point but not measured as a point.

B. Tip to Tip Spread is measured between tips of main beams.

C. Greatest Spread is measured between perpendiculars at a right angle to the center line of the
skull at widest part whether across main beams or points.

D. Inside Spread of Main Beams is measured at a right angle to the center line of the skull at widest point between main beams. Enter this measurement again in Spread Credit column if it is less
than or equal to the length of longer antler; if longer, enter longer antler length for Spread Credit.

E. Total of Lengths of all Abnormal Points. Abnormal points are those nontypical in location or
points beyond the normal pattern of five (including beam tip) per antler. Mark the points that are
normal, as defined below. All other points are considered abnormal and are entered in appropriate
blanks, after measurement in usual manner.

F. Length of Main Beam is measured from lowest outside edge of burr over outer curve to the tip of
the main beam. The point of beginning is that point on the burr where the center line along the outer
curve of the beam intersects the burr, then following generally the line of the illustration.

G-1-2-3-4. Length of Normal Points. Normal points are the brow and the upper and lower forks, as
shown in the illustration. They are measured from nearest edge of beam over outer curve to tip. Lay
the tape along the outer curve of the beam so that the top edge of the tape coincides with the top
edge of the beam on both sides of the point to determine baseline for point measurement. Record
point lengths in appropriate blanks.

H-1-2-3-4. Circumferences are taken as detailed for each measurement. If brow point is missing,
take H-1 and H-2 at smallest place between burr and G-2. If G-3 is missing, take H-3 halfway between
the base and tip of second point. If G-4 is missing, take H-4 halfway between the second point and
tip of main beam.
* * * * * * * * * * * *

FAIR CHASE STATEMENT FOR ALL HUNTER-TAKEN TROPHIES

To make use of the following methods shall be deemed as UNFAIR CHASE and unsportsmanlike and any
trophy obtained by use of such means is disqualified from entry for Awards.

   I. Spotting or herding game from the air, followed by landing in its vicinity
      for pursuit;
  II. Herding or pursuing game with motor-powered vehicles;
 III. Use of electronic communications for attracting, locating or observing
      game, or guiding the hunter to such game;
 IV. Hunting game confined by artificial barriers, including escape-proof fencing;
      or hunting game transplanted solely for the purpose of commercial shooting.
****

I certify that the trophy scored on this chart was not taken in UNFAIR CHASE as defined above by the
Boone and Crockett Club. I further certify that it was taken in full compliance with local game law
of the state, province, or territory.

Date_____Signature of Hunter_____
(Have signature notarized by a Notary Public)

For information on the Dwight Schuh Hunting Pack and other gear designed for back-country deer hunting, contact:

Eureka Pack
2711 86th Avenue E.
Puyallup, WA 98371
(206) 922-6024

For information on *Bugling for Elk, Bowhunter's Encyclopedia, Modern Outdoor Survival* and other books by Dwight Schuh, contact:

Sage Press
P.O. Box 217
Nampa, ID 83653